Solution-focused Approaches

Steve Myers

 Theory into Practice

Series Editor Neil Thompson

Russell House Publishing

First published in 2008 by:
Russell House Publishing Ltd.
4 St. George's House
Uplyme Road
Lyme Regis
Dorset DT7 3LS

Tel: 01297-443948
Fax: 01297-442722
e-mail: help@russellhouse.co.uk
www.russellhouse.co.uk

British Library Cataloguing-in-publication Data:
A catalogue record for this book is available from the British Library.

ISBN: 978-1-905541-18-8

Typeset by TW Typesetting, Plymouth, Devon

Printed by Biddles Ltd, Kings Lynn

About Russell House Publishing

Russell House Publishing aims to publish innovative and valuable materials to help managers, practitioners, trainers, educators and students.

Our full catalogue covers: social policy, working with young people, helping children and families, care of older people, social care, combating social exclusion, revitalising communities and working with offenders.

Full details can be found at www.russellhouse.co.uk and we are pleased to send out information to you by post. Our contact details are on this page.

We are always keen to receive feedback on publications and new ideas for future projects.

Contents

The Theory into Practice Series

This exciting series fills a significant gap in the market for short, user-friendly texts, written by experts, that succinctly introduce sets of theoretical ideas, relate them clearly to practice issues, and guide the reader to further learning. They particularly address discrimination, oppression, equality and diversity. They can be read either as general overviews of particular areas of theory and practice, or as foundations for further study. The series will be invaluable across the human services, including social work and social care; youth and community work; criminal and community justice work; counselling; advice work; housing; and aspects of health care.

About the Series Editor

Neil Thompson is a Director of Avenue Consulting Ltd (www.avenueconsulting.co.uk), a company offering training and consultancy in relation to social work and human relations Issues. He is also a Professor of Social Work and Well-Being at Liverpool Hope University. He has over 100 publications to his name, including best-selling textbooks, papers in scholarly journals and training and open learning materials.

Neil is a Fellow of the Chartered Institute of Personnel and Development, a Fellow of the Higher Education Academy, and the Royal Society of Arts (elected on the basis of his contribution to organisational learning). He was the founding editor of the *British Journal of Occupational Learning.* He was also responsible for setting up the self-help website, www.humansolutions.org.uk.

Series Editor's Foreword

About the series

The relationship between theory and practice is one that has puzzled practitioners and theorists alike for some considerable time, and there still remains considerable doubt about how the two interconnect. However, what is clear is that it is dangerous to tackle the complex problems encountered in 'people work' without having at least a basic understanding of what makes people tick, of how the social context plays a part in both the problems we address and the solutions we seek. Working with people and their problems is difficult and demanding work. To try to undertake it without being armed with a sound professional knowledge base is a very risky strategy indeed, and potentially a disastrous one.

An approach to practice based mainly on guesswork, untested assumptions, habit and copying others is clearly not one that can be supported. Good practice must be an *informed* practice, with actions based, as far as possible, on reasoning, understanding and evidence. This series is intended to develop just such good practice by providing:

- an introductory overview of a particular area of theory or professional knowledge;
- an exploration of how it relates to practice issues;
- a consideration of how the theory base can help tackle discrimination and oppression; and
- a guide to further learning.

The texts in the series are written by people with extensive knowledge and practical experience in the fields concerned and are intended as an introduction to the wider and more in-depth literature base.

About this book

The use of solution-focused approaches has begun to attract increasing attention in recent years, and so the publication of this book is very timely. Its clear exposition of the theoretical principles underpinning such work, combined with helpful guidance on the challenges of practice in general and of practices that challenge discrimination and oppression in particular, provides a sound foundation for high-quality practice.

The use of language in solution-focused work underlines the importance of how people make sense of their lives through the stories they and others create, echoing the concerns of one of the earlier books in the series, namely Bernard

Moss's important work on *Religion and Spirituality* (2005). Steve Myers succeeds in showing how using language constructively can be a helpful way of supporting people in developing their strengths to tackle the problems they may face in a wide range of practice settings.

This well-crafted book provides an ideal introduction to some important issues for the 'helping' professions and provides an excellent basis for developing a more advanced understanding through guidance on further reading and opportunities for learning.

Neil Thompson, Series Editor

About the author

Steve Myers is Director of The Salford Centre for Social Work Research at the University of Salford. He has worked in Community, Youth and Social Work with children and young people who have offended and their families. A lecturer in social work since 1995, he has been involved in research and evaluation into the effectiveness of interventions working with children and young people who are involved in crime. He has introduced teaching about solution-focused and narrative approaches to provide students with further tools with which to engage with service users in creative ways, and has presented at many national and international conferences and training events about these methods, as well as writing several articles about the approaches. Steve has incorporated the techniques of solution-focused approaches into his teaching, much to the bemusement of some students who are used to a problem-based approach.

Acknowledgements

As an occasional Senior Practitioner with The Junction, a Barnardo's children's service for children and young people with sexually concerning or harmful behaviours, Steve has attempted to maintain links with practice. The Junction has developed philosophies and practices influenced by solution-focused and narrative approaches that have provided a welcome (and effective) addition to thinking about how to work with problematic areas of behaviour. This book owes a debt of gratitude to the service, and in particular to the bravery and support of the service manager Lorell Webster, for allowing the creative space to explore how these practices may work in practice. Judith Milner has also provided intellectual, practical and moral support with the twist of having a relentlessly encouraging sense of humour and a tactlessness that never fails to reduce me to tears of laughter. And of course many thanks to DRWB for patience and stoicism.

Introduction

This book has its roots in the development of my own social and youth work practice, primarily with children and young people who have behaved badly in various ways, be that taking cars to joyride; stealing property from other people's homes; being violent; using illicit drugs; having difficulty with attending school or behaving sexually inappropriately. Working in voluntary and statutory social services in the UK has proved to be an often puzzling experience, as organisational demands can insist on particular practices that are demonstrably successful, yet direct contact with children, young people and their families can be saturated with problems, misery and hopelessness, leading to engagements that are riddled with conflict, anger, frustration and lack of clarity for both service users and the workers. In working with mandated and involuntary service users (referrals were mainly from the courts or child protection case conferences) there were in-built tensions about the social work role and in engaging with people with any sense of equity, partnership or collaboration. Indeed, naming people *service users* in this context was problematic as this seemed to imply a certain element of voluntary involvement (Come and use our service!) whereas the reality was that people had little or no choice (Use our service or you will go to prison, into care, into a home, into hospital!). These structural difficulties did and do not provide a context conducive to constructive partnership, making such a relationship harder to achieve and requiring skills that recognised this situation and could flexibly respond to the specific individual circumstances.

In addition to this was the imperative to prevent poor and damaging behaviours continuing, which raised tensions in using many traditional therapeutic approaches where such a directive stance can be frowned upon. Trying to find ways of working that were helpful led me to engage with the favoured theoretical positions of the day, and I have replicated these in my practice. Initially influenced by psychodynamic theory, I puzzled over the importance of early childhood experiences and the damage done to service users' attachment patterns, occasionally using Transactional Analysis to make sense of what was happening. Understanding current behaviour as a product of past psychic damage was intellectually interesting but ultimately problematic in dealing with presenting problems, as it either led to recommendations for long term psychotherapeutic care or a resignation that very little could be done given the amount of damage that people had experienced. Feminist and Marxist approaches were attractive in shifting my thinking to notions of structural power and how this may operate, but did not lead to direct practices that made much sense to the service users in terms of change. On the one hand telling boys that they were exercising their male power denied their powerlessness as children; whereas explaining their structural class disadvantages did not really give them any sense of personal agency-they were merely at the whim of materialist capitalism. Cognitive behavioural therapy (CBT) became popular in criminal justice work, making claims for effectiveness that were unassailable at the time. Concentrating on their thinking deficits and developing their social skills could be fun, but ultimately told them that they were the problem and that they were responsible for stopping their behaviour, which minimised any social influences. As the evidence for the effectiveness of CBT developed, it also became clear that this was not as solid as had been thought, so *what worked* became harder to justify.

Eventually I came across solution-focused brief therapy (SFBT) which I was initially sceptical of (not unusual for a social worker trying to work with complexities) but in practice found that they were helpful, not just for service users but for my own thinking about my practice. Since then I have incorporated these into direct practice with service users; into assessment and intervention and into teaching and learning as a social work academic and trainer. I have an engagement with narrative therapy that influences some of my understanding of the world and the similarities and differences between these approaches will be discussed later. In short, this book will be optimistic about solution-focused working, raising some potential difficulties but taking a position that these ways of working are energising, useful, rigorous and actually quite fun to use. If it appears too relentlessly positive, then so be it: the alternative is too miserable, and an unhappy worker can generate unhappy service users.

There is a range of theoretical perspectives informing work with people that make claims for understanding how people work and the required intervention to address the problems people present with. However, this position of an expert applying knowledge to help people has problems in practice, as it accentuates a divide between worker-service user and places worker analysis above that of the person who is experiencing the problems. As a youth, community and social work educator, I invited social work students in one module session to consider psychodynamic explanations for behaviour, and to think about how they could work in partnership with service users using this perspective. When I suggested that perhaps a theme of partnership was a shared understanding of the approach used by the social worker, I was met with disbelief and comments that the theory was far too complex for service users to comprehend. This formed a useful discussion about the nature of social work practice and the ways in which we can (un)intentionally take a rather superior and distant-expert position. Solution-focused approaches are based on the knowledge of the service user and therefore have the potential to be much more transparent, accessible and empowering than many other models. I will return to this theme in Part Three of this book.

How to use this book

Solution-focused brief therapy uses a range of techniques underpinned by theoretical assumptions about the way people are and what is helpful in promoting change through empowering people to take appropriate responsibility for their lives. This is an introductory book for people who wish to learn more about the theory and practice, particularly for those who wish to work in a helpful, empowering and hopeful way with people. The book provides practice examples that will be relevant to the different professional contexts of readers, as well as reflective exercises that help to illustrate how the approach works. As solution-focused work developed in therapeutic contexts many examples are drawn from encounters between workers who are counsellors in different settings and the people who come to them by various routes, whereas other examples are more specifically about social care workers going about their work in statutory and voluntary agencies with the different demands that these make. The language used within the book reflects this breadth, and I use the terms service user, client, worker and therapist as descriptors and not as judgements on the person. Increasingly, I prefer to use the term *people* for those who we come into contact with, but as we work in structures that create a divide between workers and those who we work with I have retained the distinction for clarity and as a rhetorical device. Other language use reflects the influence of solution-focused thinking, particularly words such as *helpful* and *useful* when I consider the utility of the principles and techniques described.

Part One outlines the theoretical influences on solution-focused approaches, providing the postmodern and poststructuralist context in which they have developed, as well as contrasting this with more traditional approaches. It attempts to allow the reader to think about what informs their current practice and how a solution-focused approach may be different. This will be challenging to people who hold on to strong beliefs about the nature of the world and how people *are*. I hope that it will at least provide some ideas for developing your current practice in a reflective way.

Part Two outlines the practice principles and techniques involved in solution-focused work. I have chosen to do this using an interview structure that provides some logical flow to the ideas; however, it is possible to use the techniques in different and creative ways that recognise the messy and complicated nature of practice. Indeed, some readers will be able to say that they do some of this already, which is fine. Please feel free to take away anything that may be helpful in your practice. The solution-focused techniques of the *miracle question* and *scaling* are outlined with examples of how they may be helpful in practice. In my experience many workers find these techniques accessible, straightforward and easy to use, and they lead on to doing more thinking about how the principles may be brought into everyday working practices.

Part Three outlines some of the key elements of anti-oppressive practice, an approach that has had increasing significance in practice with people in recent years. It contains a discussion of the relevance of solution-focused approaches to anti-oppressive practice, with examples of how a solution-focused approach can be used to inform anti-oppressive practice. The complexities of working with people will be familiar to readers, and this section explores how solution-focused methods can assist in acknowledging this and finding ways forward.

Part Four outlines some outcome studies and evidence for the effectiveness of solution-focused approaches, with a further section on useful websites and further reading.

Part One: The Theoretical Development of Solution-focused Approaches

Chapter 1
What are Solution-focused Approaches?

---

1. *If it ain't broke, don't fix it.*
2. *Once you know what works, do more of it.*
3. *If it doesn't work, don't do it again. Do something different.*

Miller and Berg (1995)

The above principles provide a useful starting point for SFBT, encapsulating the pragmatic and action-oriented ways of working that are a common thread within this approach. As with all ways of making sense of the world, these principles have not simply appeared, they have a developmental history influenced by individuals and ideas. This part of the book explores the context in which SFBT emerged and explores some of the theoretical constructs behind the practices.

Solution-focused approaches are ways of working that have developed from the ideas and practices of key philosophers, researchers and practitioners since the 1950s. Psychotherapy and family therapy have provided the main arenas in which such approaches have been identified, developed and thought about, but they are becoming increasingly popular in social care across the globe, particularly in the US, Canada, UK, Australasia and Scandanavia. Significant figures in the development of solution-focused work include the psychotherapist Erickson (Haley, 1967), Bateson (1972), Weakland (Weakland and Jordan, 1992) and De Shazer (1985, 1988, 1991, 1994), Berg (De Jong and Berg, 2002) and colleagues at the Brief Family Therapy Centre in Milwaukee, US. Solution-focused work is located within *brief therapies*, which are a collection of approaches that have at their heart a principle that interventions do not have to be long-term and that change can occur rapidly (hence Brief). It is often described as *solution-focused brief therapy* (SFBT), *solution oriented therapy* (Furman and Ahola, 1992) or *possibility work* (O'Hanlon, 1993). There are many different ways of working within this, with a range of practice techniques that I will return to in Part Two. These ways of working have been used with many different people presenting with many different problems, such as drug use; offending; child welfare and protection and mental health, as well as being used in a range of organisational contexts, be they statutory or voluntary, such as nursing and careers counselling (Lethem, 2002; McAllister and Moyle, 2006). The key to solution-focused approaches is *simplicity*; making sure that the processes are clear and open to all and it is in that spirit that this book attempts to provide a straightforward account of the theory and practices of solution-focused work. The SFBT acronym will be used in this book for convenience.

Parton and O'Byrne (2000) and Milner and O'Byrne (2002a) provide useful and detailed explanations of the basis of SFBT in the context of social work. SFBT is underpinned by an acknowledgement that language is of central importance, not just in interactions with people but in how the way we talk about something generates a particular understanding of it. As Parton and O'Byrne (2000, p. 97) say, 'The central principle is that talk *constructs* the future and change.' (original emphasis). Steve de Shazer (1982, 1985, 1988, 1991, 1994) undertook research into effective counselling and therapeutic practices, looking for the basic elements within a range of approaches that seemed to work. He sought to reduce the complexities of different theoretical and practical interventions to the minimum required to produce the maximum change, constructing principles and strategies for practice that would be of use to service users. In doing this he identified that future- and solution-oriented *talk* was extremely effective in assisting in constructing solutions to problems, rather than an emphasis on understanding the past and working directly with the problem which is inherent to most traditional theory and practice, particularly in social care and counselling.

However, this is not to say that this is easy or straightforward, as talking purposefully requires both discipline and skills that are often at odds with received lay and professional wisdom about how to approach working with people. In teaching and training in SFBT it is frequently the case that workers with existing theoretical knowledge struggle to set aside their desire to understand, explain and direct what should be done about problems, and find that SFBT does not fit their expectations of how a theory should operate. Most workers are encouraged to diagnose a problem; seeking root causes and applying the required intervention to modify the (usually) unwanted behaviour. SFBT does not engage in this process, which can lead to accusations that it ignores problems or does not get to the *real* problem. The theoretical justification for this will be discussed later, but the issue here is that such a different approach can be difficult to absorb as it questions long-held assumptions about such weighty matters as human nature, personality development, notions of the self and how we understand the world. It can be easier for people who have lightly held views on theory and practice to understand and apply SFBT, rather than those who have a more rigid intellectual or emotional attachment to particular theories.

Exercise 1.1

Jane is a single parent who is experiencing difficulties with providing consistent care for her two children. The children often attend school looking unkempt and when this has been raised Jane becomes very angry and confrontational with the teachers. She has spent most of her own childhood in care following physical abuse by her mother and father, and the children both have different fathers who do not play a part in their upbringing. As a black woman Jane (and her children) has received a great deal of racist abuse in the area where she lives, and also in her past when she was placed with white foster carers. Jane has recently started a relationship with another woman, Sharon, who has intermittent problems with alcohol.

- When reading this example, what range of explanations for the situation can you identify?
- Where have your explanations come from?
- How do your explanations help to inform intervention to assist Jane and her children?

Workers bring knowledge to understanding problems, but this knowledge is influenced by education and training as well as the general social environment of knowledge-production. Certain ways of understanding tend to be dominant at different times and in different professions. Therapeutic approaches also change over time, both in conceptualising people and in consequent practices, and Milner and O'Byrne (2002b), developing the ideas of O'Hanlon (1993), consider that these approaches can be broadly thought of as falling into three *waves*: pathology-based; problem-focused and solution-oriented, which can be re-envisaged as interested in the past, present and future, respectively. Workers will be familiar with the pathology-based ideas of delving into the past through the application of understandings based on psychodynamic theory, in particular the dominance of attachment theory currently in vogue in child welfare (Bowlby, 1988). These approaches locate problem behaviour as a product of influences on childhood development that have created psychic disturbance requiring responses that seek to mend this emotional hurt. The idea that people develop through a specific process and through particular stages is strong in this theory, and it is located firmly within a normative approach which views deviations from this norm as problematic (Erikson, 1948). Most adult difficulties are related to damaged internal mechanisms or delayed development, leading to practices that locate the problem within the person, hence the term pathology. Because such problems are seen as entrenched in the personality of the person, treatment becomes difficult to conceptualise and to practice due to the enormity of the task of re-structuring someone's internal world.

The second *wave* refers to the development of ideas around behaviour and cognition, concerned with observable actions of people rather than speculation about some imagined internal emotional world. Rationality and how people think are keys to these ways of working, with a focus on the presenting problems and how to deal with them directly. These approaches do not seek to understand problems through their early causality, but are more interested in the immediate run up to the problem, how it happens, and what the consequences of this are. Problems stem from dysfunctional ways of thinking and responding to situations; ways that have been learned and often repeated, compounding the difficulties. Rigid patterns of behaviour have developed that do not provide solutions to the problems, thus problems are located within the person and require expert outside assistance to recognise these deficits and to develop ways of thinking differently. Solutions are provided by the worker through illumination of the negative consequences of current thinking; developing skills to think more rationally and in suggesting ways of behaving that are more helpful. Cognitive behavioural approaches have been particularly significant in recent years, with the work of Sheldon (1995) being an example of how this approach has been claimed as the preferred evidence-supported theory for the profession.

The third *wave* of therapy moves from a focus on problems to a focus on solutions and is relatively unconcerned with the causality of problem behaviour, as such explanations can get in the way of seeking the local knowledge of the service user to construct individual solutions to the problems. Worker explanations and interpretations of problems are avoided as these may restrict the personal *agency* of the person to make sense of their world and to develop meaningful solutions *for them*. Service user strengths and successes are sought, recognised and validated and are used to work towards a problem-free future where the service user and the worker co-construct a local strategy to achieve their personal goals. The problem is seen for what it is, *a problem*, rather than being located within the emotional background, personality, traits, learned behaviour or cognitions of the person. SFBT is located within this third wave of therapeutic approaches, along with the *narrative therapy* of White and Epston (1990). It has been possible to combine SFBT and narrative therapy and Parton and O'Byrne discuss this in *Constructive Social Work* (2000) and Milner and O'Byrne (2002b) demonstrate ways of doing this creatively. The theoretical basis and associated practice of narrative therapy is helpfully outlined in detail by Payne (2006).

A SFBT approach considers that we have a tendency to focus on problems, but that this is neither necessary nor helpful in constructing *solutions*. This is a radical departure from most interventions which are past- or problem-oriented and this is not to say that these other approaches are *wrong*, but that they are based on ways of thinking that have consequences for practice that are not always helpful to the people we work with. De Shazer and his colleagues have developed a pragmatic future-oriented approach that turns most accepted theoretical methods on their head by questioning the link between past problems and future solutions by using language to assist the service user in constructing a preferred problem-free future. The act of talking about problem-free futures and how to achieve these is the key to SFBT, utilising the existing strengths and skills of the service user to develop a meaningful strategy to achieve positive change. The skill in this is not to see ourselves as identifying the problem and suggesting solutions, but in *talking constructively* with people to assist them in developing their own pathway to their preferred future. In this sense SFBT can claim to be truly empowering through its emphasis on enhancing the skills of the service user and in valuing their experience, strengths, hopes and expertise.

Exercise 1.2

- Make a mental list of all your best skills (don't be modest!).
- How do these help you to be helpful to the people you work with?
- Choose one of these skills.
- How can you enhance this skill to make it that bit more effective?
- What would you have to do?
- When can you do it by?
- How would the people you are working with know that you are doing it better?

Chapter 2
Theoretical Influences on Solution-focused Approaches

Solution-focused practices developed from research into what was effective in working with people to achieve their goals from therapy. The methods identified were not generated from a pre-existing theoretical framework, but as practitioners began to reflect on what it was that worked it became clearer that social constructionist ideas seemed to provide a useful location in which to place them. Solution-focused ways of working are a collection of practice-informed methods that have common themes of being future-oriented, strengths-based and concerned with seeking relevance for the individual being worked with, rather than led by assumptions based on pre-existing notions of how people *are*. Most theoretical perspectives have a firm sense of how people are constructed, either through personality traits, childhood experiences, social structures or a host of other influences that generate who that person is, and give pointers for understanding them and intervening in their lives. Solution-focused approaches are unconcerned with seeking a theoretical *truth* about people, and are wary of professional stories that seek to place the person into a box of theoretical explanation. This box is likely to be too limiting to fully comprehend the richness of the individual, leading to practices that focus on working with the box rather than the person.

There is debate about the very use of terminology here, as it may be more accurate to talk of solution-focused rather than Solution-Focused approaches, as to capitalise the term imparts an aura of theoretical distinctiveness that may not be the case in practice. Key figures in the development of solution-focused approaches have been De Shazer and Berg at the Milwaukee Brief Family Therapy Centre, where the ideas and practices have grown since the late 1980s out of observations and research into the effectiveness of *what worked* with people who were counselled. Rather than testing a theory or hypothesis in practice, pre-existing notions of understanding change were set aside and the focus of interest was on what was working, for whom, when and how. De Shazer in particular made claims that such pre-formed ideas of the person and what would work for them was counter-productive as it imposed a professional perspective on the person that would restrict their individuality and local strategies for change, subsuming them to the theory rather than enabling them to seek their own answers. Thus solution-focused approaches grew out of practice and are pragmatic in accepting a range of ways of working, concerned only with finding anything that will assist the person to deal with the problems that brought them into contact with services in the first place.

However, this does not mean that solution-focused practice is a complete free for all, where workers take a pick and mix or eclectic approach to practice, nor that theory does not influence it. Solution-focused approaches are influenced by broader ways of thinking about people; how they interact with their surroundings; how people are encouraged to see themselves and how we talk about something can have consequences. This latter point is central to solution-focused practices. Talking is not simply a neutral vehicle for representing an idea, how we talk can itself influence the outcome of any engagement between people. Readers will intuitively know this from their own experience: remember the feelings generated by the response of different teachers to your less than acceptable work. What style of criticism left you feeling disillusioned, miserable and worthless? What style of criticism energised you into doing better next time? Comparing the outcomes of different styles of talk in our own lives shines some light on the importance of the *way* we talk with service users. This is more than just being respectful in our conversations (although this is an intrinsic part of good practice); it is being purposeful, focused and helpful.

The rest of this chapter will discuss some of the theoretical influences on solution-focused practices. They are a product of, and influenced by, broader movements and ideas in understanding the world and these influences are reflected in the principles and practices, which will be explored in more detail in Part Two.

Social constructionism

Professional practice has been increasingly influenced by the ideas of social constructionism, and this collection of critiques has provided new ways of understanding and problematising traditional practices. It has also provided an intellectual environment that fits the principles and practices of solution-focused work and is recognised as such by key writers in the field (De Jong and Berg, 2002). The recognition that our understanding of and reaction to the world is influenced by the specific social environment in which we find ourselves is reasonably well understood and will be familiar to many professionals. This recognition has been developed through such writers as Berger and Luckman (1967) in their book *The Social Construction of Reality*, and Gergen (e.g. 1985), and has been used to provide a critique of dominant ways of working within human services. Social constructionism raises questions about the privileging of rational and scientific understandings of the world based on the explosion of critical thought in the Enlightenment period of the late eighteenth century. The discovery of science and application of scientific methods has influenced how we make sense of and work with people, but this *modernist* thinking has had some problematic consequences. Burr (2003) helpfully outlines some of the character-istics that these varied social constructionist approaches share, whilst acknowl-edging that this is not an absolute categorisation. She identifies:

1. *A critical stance towards taken-for-granted knowledge*. The dominance of certain ways of thinking mean that claims for truth are made based on traditional scientific, rational assumptions. However, these are treated scepti-cally within social constructionism and are viewed as the products of a positivist agenda that are based on the power to name something, rather than the nature of the *something* itself.
2. *Historical and cultural specificity*. What we know about the social world is often underpinned by our location in a particular place at a particular time. Our understanding of certain social *facts* changes over time and depends upon the cultural context in which we see it. An example is the way in which we view lesbian and gay people. Until 1973 the American Psychiatric Association considered homosexuality to be a psychiatric disorder, and it was only after debate and a contested vote that this was overturned. Homosexuality is now no longer (formally) considered to be a psychiatric problem, but this demon-strates the changing understanding of social phenomena, and in some cultures it is still viewed as problematic and is prohibited by extreme sanctions.
3. *Knowledge is sustained by social processes*. In social constructionist thinking, we actively generate our understandings of the world through our interactions with people and knowledge. Rather than being able to find the *real* truth of something, we construct ideas and realities through the medium of language and how we are (dis)allowed to talk about social matters. Consider a child who has been diagnosed with ADHD. Having the diagnosis can lead to a view of the child as having a medical condition that has certain deficits, yet the condition is a collection of behaviours (usually in school) that require subjective interpretation (fidgeting; disobedience; lack of concentration). The way we talk about such behaviours can lead us into different outcomes: if the child is seen as having a medical problem (ADHD) then drugs are an obvious answer; if it is seen as a problem of boredom in the classroom (too large class size) then we may look to other interventions. The explosion of ADHD diagnosis may reflect current powerful knowledge claims, rather than the *truth*.
4. *Knowledge and social action go together*. Developing the previous point, there are consequences of holding particular perspectives and understandings of the world that are influenced by structures of power. For example, if men are seen as the main perpetrators of domestic violence, then services will be provided for men who commit such acts. However, this may exclude, minimise and marginalise those women who are violent in domestic relationships, as an assumption that men are *the* problem will lead to difficulties in accepting that women can do this too, restricting services for violent women and men who

are victims. This can be seen in campaigns against domestic violence, where the victims are portrayed as women and children, but rarely men. Social constructionism views such knowledge critically, recognising that this may be a temporary truth based on particular ways of thinking and researching, rather than reflecting people's lived experiences.

The emphasis within social constructionism is that claims to certainty about people and social events are to be treated with caution, particularly where scientific methodologies produce categories and typologies in which to place people. An example that will be familiar to most students is the construction of learning styles, where certain factors are identified as indicating that people can be placed into similar groups (active *etc*) based on a notion that they have an underlying learning structure within their personality or brain. This leads to the encouragement of specific learning methods linked to these categories. However, a social constructionist critique would raise questions about how the complexities of individuals and their circumstances can be reduced into such broad groupings and resolved through rather narrow suggestions for effective learning, as well as reducing the ability to learn to a psychological matter. A student may have all the indicators of a particular learning style, but this may be of little use when faced with an environment where they have to provide child care, deal with financial problems and manage the ambivalence of their partner to their studying. Such an approach can leave students frustrated with trying to achieve their learning style when it may actually be more useful to try something that fits their *individual* situation, rather than be aggregated into a group that they share some characteristics with only some of the time.

The same principle can be applied to diagnoses of dyslexia, where learning deficits are identified and remedies are suggested, yet such assessments tend to be remarkably similar in their outcomes and propose changes that are about good teaching and learning which are relevant for all students, dyslexic or not. The act of diagnosing dyslexia can again reduce the specifics of an individual situation to a medico-psychological explanation that the problem is within the person, rather than a product of poor previous education and current teaching pressures. Of course, there are benefits from such a diagnosis, not least the financial and practical support now available, but it is ironic that the categorisation as *dyslexic* does not fit comfortably with a critical knowledge base that questions the dominance of medical scientific explanations of people. A social constructionist perspective is wary of explanations that view people as having fixed *traits* or *essences*, particularly in terms of their behaviour or personality, as these tend to have been constructed through unacknowledged theoretical assumptions and provide a label that restricts freedom of action. *Essentialist* explanations of people have practice implications. For example, The Junction Children's Service (Myers, 2003) works with *young people who have sexually harmful behaviours*, rather than *young sexual offenders*, as the former describes the range of actions committed by the young people, whereas the latter gives an identity that tends to locate the problem as part of them. Behaviours can be changed, whereas it is much harder to imagine and promote change if a person is thought of as having a fixed identity or *personality traits*.

Postmodernism

As in the debates about social constructionism, postmodernism is a collection of critiques of particular ways of thinking and can be viewed as the broader academic movement within which social constructionist ideas have flourished. Modernism was mentioned earlier; the description given to the development of the natural sciences in understanding the world through rational investigation and specific techniques. Science was seen as providing the answer to the questions about the nature of the physical world we live in, the society we inhabit and the functioning of the human body and mind. This appliance of science was privileged and raised above criticism (apart from within its own parameters), leading to approaches that claimed to find the truth of physical, social and individual matters. We can hear claims for this made today, where people can justify their arguments by stating that it is supported by scientific evidence, thus becoming more weighty and valued.

This modernist position sought underlying structures in the physical world that would explain how things worked, such as the *laws of physics*, but also applied this principle to social matters. For example, Marx developed his ideas of how societies function and change by claiming to have found underlying socio-economic patterns that explained what was happening and what would happen; identifying the inevitable emergence of particular social structures. Psychological theorists have also sought to identify underlying structures to the human personality and readers will be familiar with the work of Freud who posited the idea of the *id, ego* and *superego* as a way of understanding how people's minds functioned.

This drive to seek structures has been described as a *structuralist* approach, which is often interchangeable with a modernist position and is used as such in many texts. A further term which is linked to these modernist and structuralist ideas is that of the *grand narrative*, literally a theory (or story/way of thinking) that makes global claims about people and societies. Grand narratives tend to make claims for truth, stating that people or societies are explained by and through a particular theoretical understanding, and have a determinist and inevitable element to them. Individuals are subsumed into these stories and their sense of personal agency (or the ability to make choices or determine their own identity) is marginalised. In professional practice there are often grand narratives at work when service users are storied as the inevitable victims of socio-economic factors beyond their control, such as living in poverty and deprivation, where expectations of people are limited by notions of *class*, making it difficult for them to assert their personal experience and strengths. The grand narrative reduces people to pawns who are at the whim of forces beyond their control.

Another example is Erikson's (1948) stages of human development, where people are assumed to have to go through various life stages to achieve a harmonious existence. This story talks about how these stages are to be successfully negotiated and the problems associated with failing to accept or move through these. As an explanation it may have some intuitive merit, but the consequences of this way of thinking lead to a value judgement on how people choose to act and live their lives, based on normative western white male heterosexual middle class expectations. When subjected to this model many people are found to be lacking, and difference is constructed as deviance and deficit. Thus there are dangers in holding onto rigid structural explanations of how people *should* be which are important for practice.

Parton and O'Byrne (2000, p. 19) summarise the key features of modernity as being:

- The understanding of history as having a definite and progressive direction (as in the theories of Marx).
- The attempt to develop universal categories of experience (as in the concepts developed by Freud).
- The idea that reason can provide a basis for all activities (applying scientific methods to understanding social events).
- The idea that the nation state could coordinate and advance such developments for the whole society (as in the construction of the welfare state).

Modernity seeks to establish truth and absolute knowledge, assuming that this is hidden beneath the surface of events and requiring investigation to uncover the reality. In professional practice this can often take the form of being encouraged to look behind the presenting problems for the underlying difficulties, with metaphors such as *peeling away the layers* being used to indicate that there is a core being that would benefit from discovery. This places the worker in the position of being an expert diagnostician, applying theories and methods to inform the service user what is wrong with them and how to remedy this. Indeed, within the modernist framework the professional is privileged with having the tools to determine the truth and reality of a situation, be that in biology, engineering, medicine or social care. The service user becomes an *object* of investigation, viewed as some *thing* to make sense of through expert knowledge, marginalising the lived experience of the service user into professional constructions.

Postmodernism (and the related concept poststructuralism) has questioned the above assumptions about underlying structures and processes that are central to modernism and structuralism (Foucault, 1988; Peters, 1999). Rather than viewing the search for such over-arching explanations as being a straight-forward scientific investigation, it has rejected the very idea of this method, seeing it as a product of a particular way of thinking about the world. The application of natural scientific methods to understanding social events and people is problem-atic, as is the assumption that grand narratives and global explanations truly exist and simply need to be found. Postmodernist thinking views people as being much more fragmented, fluid, contradictory and complex than a modernist approach would be able to accept. The very idea of the existence of an underlying structure is viewed as a product of dominant ways of thinking, rather than an absolute and real truth. Modernism is critiqued for hiding value judgements and privileged perspectives behind unacknowledged positions of power, prioritising particular claims for truth over others that are marginalised.

The certainties of modernism have been questioned, in particular the notion that social progress is linear and inevitable. There is recognition within post-modernity that old certainties have been eroded and that there are many different ways of understanding the world that can have claims to be true in their context. On one level this can be seen in changing patterns of employment, as I am of a generation that can remember when working class men were expected to enter industrial work at sixteen and remain within this for the rest of their working lives, providing the income for their families and assuming specific gendered roles within this. Cleary this pattern has dissolved as work opportunities have changed and such assumptions have been removed through economic and social changes. The former assumptions about life courses and roles have changed beyond recognition, providing opportunities as well as reducing the security previously offered (Rosenau, 1992; Bauman, 1993). Life has become much more fragmented, not simply in its lived experience, but in how we think about our role in society.

Smart (1999) talks of how the postmodern condition leads us to have to engage with ambivalence and uncertainty, recognising that differences exist and that many social matters are relative rather than absolute. Diversity is more readily accepted and validated as questions are raised about the modernist tendency to impose explanations from positions of power. Instead of truth uncovered through rationality, we have the possibility of many truths depending on where people are situated. For example, social work has traditionally been situated within the modernist agenda (Fook, 2002), but this has been increasingly questioned, and the importance of recognising that practice is always contingent and uncertain has become key to current debates about the nature of the profession (Parton and O'Byrne, 2000). Solution-focused approaches can be seen to be within this general movement, through their concern with the individual, how that person understands and interacts with the world, their local resources and their personal situation.

The importance of language

A consequence of postmodern and poststructuralist thinking has been the recognition that *how* we talk is in itself important in generating understandings and realities. The work of poststructuralist writers on language has opened new opportunities to reflect on the processes of interactions between people. We have already seen that truth is something that is open to interpretation and that there is doubt that any claim to truth is value-free or neutral. This is also the case in the ways that we represent matters through language, where the words and grammar we use are not simply a direct representation of a solid fact, but actually have their own life in generating a particular understanding of this supposed fact. Language plays a part in constructing our realities, as we go about trying to describe matters within the restraints, boundaries and rules of the language we choose to use. Besley (2002, p. 128) states:

> Both the language and how it is used are important. Language can blur, alter or distort experience as we tell our stories; it can condition how we think, feel, and act and can be used purposefully as a therapeutic tool.

The direct connection between words and what they are meant to represent has been destabilised in this approach, as it has been recognised that how a matter is talked about actively creates it, thus different ways of talking can create different understandings of the same supposed fact (Derrida, 1978). If talk is productive, then it can be harnessed in ways to produce desired outcomes when working with people.

The context in which we talk heavily influences understanding, so within this way of thinking people define their identities through processes of interaction with the social world and other individuals, and rather than having fixed inner traits or core identities we construct and re-construct who we are and our sense of the world all the time. For example, having a personality type or specific learning style can be seen to be less a reflection of reality and more a product of dominant ways of talking and understanding. Potter and Wetherell (1987) argue that how we talk about social events does not simply represent these, but constructs a version of those events, through the boundaries imposed by language and its impact on the range of imaginable and acceptable explanations. The philosopher Wittgenstein (1963) identified that knowledge, or what we know (or what we think we know) about the world is mediated through language games, thus our realities are produced *by and through* language, rather than language simply reflecting what we know.

We enter into conversations with ourselves and others purposefully, seeking to utilise ways of talking that are persuasive, rather than necessarily reflecting fact. How we talk will affect the strength of our arguments and the solidity of our views, thus the *rhetoric* used is as important (indeed if not more so) as the content of discussions. As Rorty (1979, p. 359) states: 'the way things are said is more important than the possession of truths'. Talking is a dynamic act that opens and closes possibilities for change. It is this recognition of the generative nature of language that underpins solution-focused approaches; where what is said, when it is said and how it is said are all key aspects of the methods involved. Using language *itself* as a tool to create change is unlike most therapeutic approaches which consider language merely as a way of reflecting or describing the truth of a person. O'Connell (2001, p. 29) says that unlike structurally-based theorists, solution-focused workers:

> ... explore not what is within (intrapsychic) people, as if there was an inner world divorced from a cultural, anthropological context, but to examine what lies between people, i.e. an interactional perspective. Feelings, thoughts and actions always take place within the linguistic negotiations in which people engage. Meanings are always open for renegotiation.

Thus words are powerful in that they can create bias and are based on assumptions about the nature of people and problems. O'Hanlon (1993) discussed the ways in which workers can inadvertently close down options and accentuate problems through their use of language, which has been described as *iatrogenic injury*, that is, harm caused by treatment (Parton and O'Byrne, 2000, p. 56). O'Hanlon argues that interventions in people's lives should follow principles of *iatrogenic healing* by being respectful and opening up possibilities for change.

Practice Example 2.1

David was a young man who had experienced major adversities in his life, having been rejected by his parents at an early age and subsequently placed in a bewildering range of unsuccessful foster placements. Now seventeen, he was lonely, miserable, struggling to make friends and self-harming, with little sense of how he could change his life. He was referred to a specialist project for isolated young people and was seen by James, a worker who had trained in attachment theory. After listening to David describe his problems and feelings, James shared with David that he thought that his problems stemmed from the difficulties of his childhood which had created ways of being that were deep-rooted, and that his training and experience led him to believe that David could resolve his problems but that it would take at least two years of weekly therapy exploring his past to achieve this. David appreciated the help offered but found it difficult to imagine committing to such a long-term project and became pre-occupied with his past experiences. His self-harming became more pronounced.

Solution-focused approaches recognise that what we say (words, phrases, concepts) and how we say it (tone, pitch, statement or question, associated body language) can affect the experience of the conversation and that this will impact on people in different ways. The above example, which is not embellished, demonstrates how assumptions about people's problems and their treatment can actually generate further hopelessness. The talk was about problems and their assumed theoretical nature, and confirming that the root cause was within the person and their (unchangeable) past. This makes change hard to envisage, whereas talk that is about solutions can actually generate the environment, motivation and possibility of change. I will return to the theme of language in Chapter 10, looking in more detail about how this is important for anti-oppressive practice.

Exercise 2.1

- Think of a small problem you have been experiencing
- When has the problem been less of a problem?
- What was happening when the problem was less?
- What were you doing when the problem was less?
- How did you do this?
- Well done! How can you do more of it?

Chapter 3
Differences Between Traditional and Solution-focused Approaches

The different *waves* of therapeutic interventions outlined in Chapter 1 identified that there has been a development away from problem and past-focused counselling towards solution and future-oriented approaches. Current practice in therapy, counselling and general people-work is heavily weighted towards the problem-focused models, such as psychodynamic and cognitive-behavioural approaches. These have been influential for so long that they are often taken for granted and can be argued to have become traditional ways of working. Solution-focused approaches are a radical break with these traditional practices and it is worth outlining the differences between them.

Milner and O'Byrne (2002b, p. 13) argue that:

> . . . solution talk cannot easily be combined with problem-focused counselling in some sort of 'add on' way in certain cases, as an entirely different set of principles is involved based on a fundamentally different way of understanding people.

They helpfully outline key differences between traditional, modernist ways of conceptualising and practising, and those of a solution-focused approach.

Accepting people's experiences

Many engagements with service users are underpinned by discussions to establish the truth of the situation, informed by professional knowledge that seeks to get to the root or reality of the problem. SFBT is more concerned with listening to the person and hearing their explanations and sense-making of the situation, questioning for detail about the local experience of the person and avoiding premature decisions that the problem has been identified. In my work with children and young people with sexual behaviour problems, there has been an assumption that this behaviour can be explained through their cognitive deficits or distortions, thus leading to questioning that searches for these factors, in order to provide a template for intervention. However, a solution-focused approach is much more interested in the local story of how the person deals with and makes sense of this behaviour, with an emphasis on ways forward.

Practice Example 3.1

John came to a specialist project for his sexual misbehaviour following a period in a residential unit for sexual abusers. He stated that he was a sex offender and could articulate the cognitive distortions that had been identified during his previous treatment. The work with him began by asking him to identify all those aspects of himself that were not like a sex offender, and what it might take for him to no longer be called a sex offender. This was puzzling for him as he had been co-constructed as someone with sex offender traits that he felt were part of him. He was able to develop a sense of himself as having the possibility of having a problem-free future, rather than constantly being on guard against his sex offender traits.

Searching for solutions

SFBT is not interested in the causality or nature of problems, but is concerned with seeking solutions to difficulties. Wittgenstein (1963) questioned the assumption that we need to understand problems in order to construct answers, and SFBT takes the position that focusing on problems can generate further difficulties, including a sense of being stuck in the past. As Beckett (2006, p. 73) helpfully says: 'In behavioural terms, most traditional approaches to therapy *reward* problem talk with sympathy and attention and therefore *reinforce* the behaviour of 'problem talking'. De Shazer's approach reinforces solution talking (original emphasis)'. Indeed, De Shazer (1991, p. xiii) explicitly states that 'The solution is not necessarily related to the problem' which questions many current assumptions about practice.

Practice Example 3.2

During assessment to be a foster carer, Sharon was asked questions about her sexual abuse as a child and how this may have damaged her capacity to provide the care and protection required for any children. She had to demonstrate that she had resolved these problems, yet she had been getting on with her life perfectly adequately in her own way. The act of raising this matter generated anxiety and it was based on professional understandings of the nature of emotional damage, rather than focusing on the way she had developed her own strategies to deal with the abuse. A solution-focused approach would be interested in talking about future solutions, rather than asking why something has happened.

In workshops about SFBT I have invited participants to provide explanations for particular behaviours which can generate a long list of reasons, all of which are perfectly reasonable and based on theoretical knowledge, yet often so varied that it would be difficult to make sense of how they could all inform intervention. Solution-focused work accepts that *things happen* and that when we provide an explanation we are actually simply having a professional guess that does not always provide helpful answers. For example, if someone is diagnosed as having an attachment disorder (Bowlby, 1988), this does not necessarily lead to easy treatment options, and becomes a fixed identity that can hold back any expectation of progress and change. Given a choice between understanding a problem or finding a solution, most people seem to wish to choose the latter, despite strong cultural and theoretical messages that we need to *unpack the real problem* in order to find solutions.

A focus on competencies

The side-stepping of problems is not to ignore them (and indeed people often want to talk about them), it simply views them as unhelpful in co-constructing solutions. SFBT views the strengths and competencies that people have as being the keys to developing change away from the problem. The problem is rarely always present; there are times when it does not occur, or when it is less problematic. People are often overwhelmed by or subsumed into the problem, reinforced by theories that take the problem as their focus without recognising that people will have capabilities that are marginalised, neglected or hidden by such an approach. Asking people to talk about their good qualities and what they are doing when things are OK can be a surprise to service users, who often expect to talk about problems and have already accepted that they are likely to be part of the problem. Service users can be asked to list their good points and what is going right in their lives, which sadly some people find difficult to do due to their perception of themselves. It is a skill of the SFBT practitioner to enable people to identify and develop these points, as they provide the basis of a strategy to develop a problem-free life.

In a recent research project talking with women who were experiencing severe and multiple deprivations, we constructed an interview schedule that began by asking them to tell us about what they and their children were good at. This generated a great deal of surprise and laughter and encouraged people to engage in a process of thinking about their circumstances and what had been helpful for them. This was used in preference to the original question which was more focused on the problems they had experienced. Information came out in a much richer way, rather than simply as a catalogue of misery. If people struggle to think of anything positive about themselves, then they can be asked to go and talk to other people to see what positives they can see in them. Judith Milner (personal communication) even suggests that people can go and ask their dog, to imagine what good qualities they see in their owner. This helps to overcome the difficulty of sometimes being seen by others as a total problem, or provides a game to rehearse asking other people sometimes embarrassing questions about themselves.

Focusing on what people want to talk about

Many traditional approaches locate problems and solutions in the past, seeking to explore what has happened in order to understand what has gone wrong. Solution-focused approaches avoid the past except where it may be helpful to use previous successes to inform future strategies. The emphasis is on allowing the person to talk about what is important for them, rather than asking questions based on theoretical or professional assumptions that will lead the conversation in the preferred way of the interviewer. Professional practice tends to hypothesise about the nature of problems and then seek confirmation (or disconfirmation) of this, which may marginalise the local experience of the person. Encouraging someone to talk about their understanding of what is happening is important, as this helps to avoid premature decisions that fit the worker's assumptions.

Cognitive behavioural approaches, for example, will explore the nature of the problem behaviour by looking at the antecedents, what happened and the consequences, trying to identify how the person has made 'faulty' decisions that can then be rectified (Sheldon, 1995). This assumes that people have this problem inside them, and questions will be focused on seeking problem-supporting thinking. The idea that we can change through analysis of past events is a strong cultural one supported by theoretical models, but SFBT does not accept that this is always the case, and that such a preoccupation with the past can actually hamper constructing solutions. Many service users expect to talk about the past, as our society is riddled with cultural notions of disclosure and introspection (bolstered by chat shows and magazine quizzes) that promote this model. The solution-focused practitioner will respect this but raise questions about the usefulness for the person, allowing them to consider how the past can really assist in building the future.

Focusing on behaviour rather than emotions

Feelings are central to most professional practice, where sensitivity to service users is often constructed as engaging with emotions. Solution-focused work does not ignore emotions, but it is interested in detail and process, so asking people how they 'do' particular emotions is useful. Consider love for instance; how do you demonstrate that you love someone? What do you do? Parents may say that they love their children, and indeed in our society we place a great deal of value in providing a loving environment, but what is useful to know is how this is done, as otherwise the term remains vague and many different interpretations could be made of it. Turnell and Lipchick (1999) argue that because SFBT is interested in the particular and individual circumstances of the person, this is experienced as being heard, which can be viewed as empathic. Empathy is demonstrated through *actions* of respect, listening and remaining focused on the lived experience of the person.

SFBT views behaviours as able to be quantified in a way that is difficult with emotions, so if someone says that they feel better, then they would be asked about when they feel better; how they feel better and what it takes to feel better. Models such as a psychodynamic approach focus strongly on emotions, yet these are linked to past events that can neither be changed nor necessarily provide ways forward and can be very hard to engage with. For example, professional care workers often talk about service users having *low self-esteem*, with roots in early childhood experiences (poor attachments being the current favoured explanation), yet self-esteem is a complex interaction of personal, familial and social influences that would benefit from specificity for that person. So in a SFBT approach, rather than viewing the person having low self-esteem as a complete and totalising label, details about when the person feels good (when is their self-esteem OK?), how this happens (what is happening when they are feeling better than usual) and what makes people have less poor self-esteem (what or who helps them to feel good about themselves?) would be action/behaviour-oriented questions to ask.

Avoiding diagnosis, categorisation and pathology

Despite some protestations to the contrary, most traditional approaches tend to be based on a process of diagnosis and categorisation, leading to the pathologising of service users. Workers apply their theoretical knowledge to analysing the problem, finding out the true nature of it, and making recommendations for intervention based on what is known to be the indicated intervention or treatment. For example, a cognitive behavioural approach would seek to identify cognitive distortions and then work with these based on models of change, listing triggers of the behaviour, thinking deficits and looking at different ways of managing the patterns of problem behaviour. This tends to locate the problem *within* the person and inevitably leads to the pathologisation of people (George *et al.*, 2000).

Solution-focused approaches are not interested in this process, viewing it as a way of thinking that may be of use to certain professionals but unhelpful in constructing problem-free futures. Indeed, the process of diagnosis can create its own problems, as it closes down the multitude of options that may be available to the person's local situation. Instead, by focusing on a person's strengths this pathologising process is avoided.

Practice Example 3.3

Mrs Smith, who had reached the age of 82, had a fall at home that raised concerns about her safety in the community as a *frail elderly person*. She was asked questions about how she had been managing to live independently, what skills she had developed to maintain her independence, how she had managed crises before, what she felt would be useful services to assist her to maintain her independence and what qualities she had that would help her to achieve this. Mrs Smith was able to say what she wanted and needed to return home safely, which resulted in a package of support that fitted her personality and lifestyle, rather than focusing on assumptions about her frailty.

Milner and O'Byrne (2002b, p. 16) provide a helpful medical metaphor for use with people who may be puzzled by this different approach, particularly when professionals and service users expect problems to be at the centre of discussions:

> . . . you can ask them which they would prefer: root and branch surgery on the problem or a boost to their immune system so that their mind and body can deal with the problem painlessly?

This playfully demonstrates the differences between the traditional medical model of approaching a problem and the solution-focused emphasis on strengths.

Being respectfully uncertain

Insight and inference are key aspects of traditional approaches where practitioners are encouraged to look into the facts of the person and to draw inferences from their behaviour and emotions. However, insight tends to be outsight, in the sense that it is someone looking from the outside in and making judgements. We *infer* from our conversations and pre-existing knowledge what is going on for that person. This is obviously open to misunderstanding, as what the practitioner may *think* is happening may only be a reflection of their own values and knowledge. A solution-focused worker would resist making assumptions and would check out with the person exactly what they mean, rather than being certain that they have got it right. The explanations people have for their behaviour are listened to respectfully, but this does not necessarily mean that they are accepted uncritically. Questions can be asked to encourage people to tell us more, so that the story is unpacked in further detail.

Practice Example 3.4

James was a boy who had been violent, and a worker was concerned when James talked about how he thought that rape was worse than murder, as this seemed to downplay serious violence and to suggest a lack of empathy. However, when asked further questions about his reasoning behind this, it became clear that James felt that women had to live with the consequences of rape for the rest of their lives, whereas murder was an end event. What emerged through questioning was a boy who did have the capacity to view the consequences of his actions for others and this was a useful start to exploring how he could avoid creating victims of his violence in the future.

A respectfully uncertain approach would listen carefully to what people had to say and delay judgement on this, seeing any explanation as being contingent, temporary and subject to change. Workers often come across people who have experienced *trauma*, a term that is usually applied when a significant negative event has occurred to someone, such as abuse, neglect or any other harmful behaviour. Trauma is another term that is rather woolly and encompasses a huge variation of events and their specifics for the person involved, but these are subsumed into this singular construct. This can lead to expectations of how someone should process and deal with trauma, without necessarily exploring the meaning for that particular person (Butt, 2004). It is common to describe people who do not wish to talk about their adverse life events as being *in denial*, which is pathologising their choice not to talk. Bowlby (1998, p. 153) says that if someone is critical of therapy or misses a session then 'a therapist who adopts attachment theory would ask himself [*sic*] why his patient is afraid to express his feelings openly and what his childhood experiences may have been to account for his distrust'. SFBT, however, may consider that the therapy is not working for the person or that they may not have the money to get the bus. Solution-focused workers would not enforce nor judge what a person chooses to talk about, but would encourage discussion about what is important for them.

Practice Example 3.5

A young girl was sexually assaulted by a stranger. She was referred to a group for girls who had been sexually abused, run by a local support organisation. The girl went to the first meeting but there were concerns about her contribution and her unwillingness to participate and *open up*, leading to concerns that she was *bottling things up* and was *in denial* of the damage the assault had done to her. This was obviously of concern, but when asked about her experiences of the group it became clear that all the other girls were there because of the long-term sexual abuse by close family members, whereas her concerns were different as her assailant had been a stranger, it was a one-off event, she had told her family immediately who had supported her and the assailant had been quickly arrested, charged and dealt with by the courts. She had been subsumed into a *sexual abuse victim* story that did not fit her specific circumstances, and was beginning to be pathologised by her rejection of the proffered treatment.

Avoiding blame

People often make sense of problems by blaming themselves, attributing adverse events to their personal failings. This is linked to notions of how to 'be' in society; for example, motherhood has strong social prescriptions attached to it that can be unattainable all of the time. Those readers who have children will be able to remember those times when you wondered just where you went wrong and that there is a strong normative drive telling you exactly what a *good mother* should be doing. Trying to live up to this is extremely demanding and exhausting, and probably doomed to failure, but rather than view this as the inevitable product of unrealistic gendered expectations and a society that provides limited support for mothers, there is a tendency to see this as an individual deficit. This can be (often unintentionally) reinforced by professional interventions.

Practice Example 3.6

Shaheen and her children left her abusive husband and were supported by a women's project. She undertook group work designed, in the words of the workers, to assist her in developing her skills and confidence to resist entering into other abusive relationships. This located the problem not in her husband's behaviour or social expectations, but in her personal attributes, making her feel at least partly responsible for the abuse she had suffered.

SFBT avoids entering into blame territory by focusing on the *good* attributes of a person, along with their strengths and achievements, which side-steps the difficulties created by problem-talk. This is not to say that responsibility is avoided, and as Milner and O'Byrne (2002b, p. 16) say, 'It is much more fruitful to look at behaviour in terms of responsibility taking', particularly in the future. Responsibility is different from blame in that it is about a person developing or recognising their agency and choices, within sensible boundaries. It is unfair and unreasonable to expect an eight-year-old child to take full responsibility for their actions, but it *is* reasonable to ask an adult to think about how they can take responsibility for their future behaviour. *Blame* freezes people into inactivity, passivity and powerlessness, whereas *responsibility* recognises capacity, change and context.

The role of the worker

Most professional interventions position the worker as the expert entering into people's lives to make sense of a problem, be that using a preferred theoretical perspective or a prescribed assessment protocol. The worker using SFBT is an expert in the techniques and processes required to assist the person to seek their own solutions, rather than an expert in telling people what the problem is and what solutions are recommended. Skills in communication are central to this and if there is any *real* expert in SFBT it is the person themselves, who has all the knowledge about their history, previous achievements, how the problem has been managed so far and what might work in the future.

> ### Practice Example 3.7
>
> John had been involved in a series of fights with other men, leading to a description of him as *violent*. A cognitive behavioural approach was taken towards his behaviour that sought to identify his cycle of aggression, including triggers, cognitive distortions and reinforcers. He struggled to see how his behaviour fitted this model and was in danger of being labelled as *resistant* and *in denial*. A solution-focused worker began to ask him about the times when the problem was not a problem, and what was happening when he was not being violent, which was most of the time. This approach enabled James to think about how he could use those times when he had acted responsibly to resist the problem behaviour. He was able to work out his own plan to demonstrate his increased responsibility and to reduce the opportunities to behave badly. He began to see what had worked well previously and to do more of this, producing a complicated, specific and individual plan.

Jackson and McKergow (2002, p. 7) provide a useful summary of the differences between Problem-focused and Solution-focused approaches:

Problem Focus	Solution Focus
The Past	The Future
What's Wrong	What's Working
Blame	Progress
Control	Influence
The Expert knows best	Collaboration
Deficits	Resources
Complications	Simplicity
Definitions	Actions

> ### Exercise 3.1
>
> - Looking at the above comparisons, can you think of times when you have worked with people in both problem-focused and solution-focused ways?
> - Try and remember the best interview you have ever done with someone as a worker or student.
> - How did you do this?
> - What elements of the above lists were present?

O'Connell (1998, p. 21) provides an excellent outline of solution-focused theory and practice in counselling, providing a helpful comparison of the sort of questions and conversations that arise from the above differences:

Problem Focused Questions	Solution-focused Questions
How can I help you?	How will you know when therapy has
Could you tell me about the problem?	been successful?
Is the problem a symptom of	What would you like to change?
something deeper?	Have we clarified the central issue on
Can you tell me more about the	which you want to concentrate?
problem?	Can we discover exceptions to the
How are we to understand the problem	problem?
in the light of the past?	What will the future look like without the
How many sessions will be needed?	problem?
	Have we achieved enough to end?

Exercise 3.2

- In reflecting on the above lists, what differences can you see in the way in which the questions are phrased?
- What sort of questions do you use in your current practice?
- Which of your questions have been the most useful for the service users?
- Which of your questions have been most useful for you as a professional worker?

Part Two: Practice Principles, Assumptions and Techniques

This section of the book explores the practice principles and assumptions within SFBT, looking at how the key issues of empathy, listening, problem-free talking, transparency and brevity are conceptualised within the model. These principles and assumptions are important in making sense of the practices, providing the rationale for ways of working that may seem unusual to people who have been influenced by more traditional approaches. The section then outlines the main techniques that have been developed to achieve effective, useful change. Finding exceptions (the times when the problem was less of a problem); strengths (which are often neglected) and developing clear goals (which are measurable and achievable) are outlined, including the use of *scales* and the *miracle question*, which are central tools for the solution-focused worker.

The structure broadly follows the process of an interview with a service user, although the techniques can be used in different ways at different times, or even extracted and used wherever a worker thinks they may be helpful. Examples from a range of situations will assist the reader in making connections with their practices.

Chapter 4
Practice Principles and Assumptions

SFBT is underpinned by hypotheses about people and interventions that provide the backdrop to all of the practice techniques used in the approach. These principles and assumptions form a useful platform on which to build individualised practice for service users, enabling workers to reflect on how their specific work is maintaining the required rigour and values involved. These have proved to be helpful, particularly given the professional, cultural and theoretical dominance of problem-focused approaches that workers are often saturated with. The desire to *know* about a problem is deeply embedded and I can recall many times when I have pondered over the nature of the difficulties a service user has brought, only to find that I was often wrong (or at best partially right some of the time) or that this did not provide me or the person with any individual strategy for change.

Vinnicombe (2004) and Milner and O'Byrne (2002a, p. 139) provide lists of key assumptions as an aid to practice. The following is a synthesis of their points.

Assumptions about problems

- The problem is the problem; the service user is not the problem
- Problems do not necessarily indicate a personal deficit
- Problems happen in interactions between people rather than inside them
- Problems are not always present; exceptions occur
- Complicated problems do not always require a complicated solution

Assumptions about the past

- Events just happen: exploring the past leads to blame whereas the goal is to develop responsibility for the future
- Exploring a problem-free future avoids having to dwell on or understand the past
- A diagnosis does not have to determine the future

Assumptions about change

- Change always happens; nothing stays the same
- What may appear to be small changes can be hugely significant
- Change can be constructed through talk

Assumptions about talking

- Hearing what the service user has to say is important
- Take a *not-knowing* stance that reduces premature and imposed worker judgement
- Stay on the surface of conversations rather than looking beneath; any search for meaning is likely to be the worker's interpretation
- People experience and make sense of their world in different ways; their reality may not be yours

Assumptions about solutions

- Identify what is going right rather than what is going wrong
- Service users have the solutions to the problems; assist them in finding these
- Solutions generated by the service user are more likely to be meaningful, achievable and successful
- Imposing *what works* for others does not always work for the individual; seek what works for them
- Increasing service user choices will enable behaviour change
- Goals need to be meaningful for the service user in order to be successful, but they also need to be legal and moral

The above assumptions permeate the practice techniques that will follow. They may raise questions for practitioners about your understanding of the world, and indeed many people consider some of the assumptions to be rather shallow and in opposition to notions of what constitute the professional role in practice. However, I would invite people to set aside these preconceived ideas and embrace some of the ways of working; to practise some of the practices to see how they may work for your service users and for you. The assumptions may well appear shallow to theoretical positions that have a working hypothesis about the existence of *depth*: let us compromise and say that SFBT is *deeply shallow* as it takes a surface stance that is supported by the theoretical and philosophical perspectives previously outlined.

Practice principles

Good professional practice is based on values of respect for the individual and the importance of behaving sensitively with the difficulties and distresses that people are experiencing (Biestek, 1957). Research into therapy indicates that the nature of the client-therapist (service user-worker) relationship, whatever the theoretical perspective taken, is a major factor in the success or otherwise of the encounter (Hubble *et al.*, 1999). Rarely do people engage with services unless there is some perceived problem, either by their own assessment or by that of others. Trying to maintain a respectful stance underscores solution-focused approaches and this is demonstrated in various ways. Turnell and Edwards (1999, p. 29), when applying SFBT in child protection cases, emphasise the need to 'Respect service recipients as people worth doing business with', rather than doing things to, which can be difficult where a child is suspected of being maltreated but is a position of partnership and hope. Sharry *et al.* (2003) explicitly call this developing a *therapeutic alliance*, making comparisons between the worker-service user relationship in SFBT and the values of unconditional positive regard in the writing of Rogers (1986).

Empathy

Social care and counselling practice often considers *empathy* to be a central feature of any therapeutic intervention, influenced by Rogers' (1957, p. 99) definition of this as being able to 'sense the client's private world as if it were your own, but without ever losing the 'as if' quality' and 'to sense the client's anger, fear or confusion without getting bound up in it'. This understanding of empathy often encourages workers to demonstrate that they have *felt the pain* of the service user, thus giving insight into their world and allowing the worker to reflect this understanding back to the service user. In doing this it is claimed that the service user feels more understood and is more likely to open up to telling more about their difficulties. The notion of empathy has raised debates within SFBT about what it is and how it is expressed (Turnell and Lipchik, 1999), not least based on research evidence that questions the value of empathy as a significant factor in successful therapeutic outcomes (Lambert and Bergin, 1994).

The idea of active listening to elicit empathic responses can itself be a rather artificial and worker-led construction which singles out emotions as the focus of work. Miller and De Shazer (2000) questioned the need to do this, as it could lead to imposing emotion-talk when the service user may not wish to do this, with the added danger that it could locate current problems within their emotions thus leading to blame and pathology. Separating out emotions pre-supposes that they exist outside the social and interpersonal context, whereas a solution-focused understanding of emotions places them within behaviour which is performed, thus leading to questions about how people *do* emotions (sadness; hurt; joy; love) rather than how they *feel*. Empathy is a complex matter which can only be demonstrated through actions (words; sounds; movements), but SFBT avoids some of the more sentimental and problem-focused statements associated with demonstrating a traditional notion of empathy. De Jong and Berg (2002, p. 41) recommend avoiding statements that intend to confirm the service user's feelings, but that actually reinforce the unhappiness people may be experiencing, such as 'You're really hurting now. This seems to be a deeply discouraging time in your life'. The intention of such a response may be genuinely meant to demonstrate understanding, but actually feeds into a notion of helplessness and hopelessness.

SFBT is not a cold and clinical approach that ignores emotions (although it is criticised as such by those who hold a particular view of what empathy should be), but it validates and understands them in different ways than a more traditional perspective and expresses empathy differently. It does it with what O'Hanlon (1995) calls a *twist*, acknowledging the feelings but using language to explore possibilities for difference and change, developing the traditional concept of empathy into *empathy plus*. If someone says that they *cannot cope any more*, a solution-focused worker may say 'It sounds really difficult at the moment. What was happening when you were coping previously?' Or if a parent and child say that they are *not getting on, always fighting and shouting*; then a solution-focused response may be to say that 'I can see that you are not getting on now. Can you tell me about the times when you have got on?' Or if someone says that their life *has been dreadful, I hurt all the time because I was abused*, then a response could be to say 'That sounds awful and it is brave of you to come here and talk. Can you tell me what you hope to gain through having the courage to come here?' It would be callous in the extreme to completely ignore the strength of emotion that people feel and it is important to remember that SFBT is solution-*focused*, not solution-*forced* (Nylund and Corsiglia, 1994). Sharry *et al.* (2003, p. 18) warn that 'Many novice therapists, in their desire to be solution-focused, may rush straight ahead to goaling and solution building without having first listened to or connected with their clients.' To seek solutions relentlessly when someone is expressing grief or pain at events that have severely impacted on their emotional well-being is not helpful in developing a cooperative relationship, but nonetheless the validation can be expressed in such a way as to sow the seeds of exceptions, agency and change.

Listening

One of the key actions that underpins respecting service users is that of listening, which is true of most approaches to working with people. In SFBT this takes the form of listening with *solution building ears* (De Jong and Berg, 2002, p. 21) in order to seek clues for a problem-free future. SFBT uses the traditionally helpful listening skills that are common to many therapeutic interventions, such as open questions, the use of non-verbal behaviours, summarising and paraphrasing, but builds on these. Listening in professional practice has traditionally been focused on finding out the true nature of the problem based on the preferred theoretical perspective of the worker or agency, thus filtering information through the worker's framework. This is not surprising, as we tend to make judgements on what people are saying all the time, evaluating and trying to make sense of the information given. This *deeper* analysis leads to difficulties, as in a case where a mother who had experienced domestic violence and sexual abuse in the past was refusing to allow her daughter to go out of the house without rather strict conditions. The speculation was that she was transferring some of her unresolved feelings about her experiences onto her daughter, and that work would be needed to be done to assist her in coming to terms with these. After further questioning it emerged that there had been an increase in racist violence in the area and mother was concerned that her (black) daughter may be subjected to this. Rather than being a pathology-based problem, this was actually a rather sensible precaution to the very real threat to her daughter which required action in the local community to enhance safety.

Research into professional decision-making confirms that there is a tendency to make an initial judgement which becomes the marker for all further speculation, with subsequent information being framed to support the original hypothesis (e.g. Sinclair et al., 1995). This *rush to judgement* can be influenced by agency needs, but is also the product of various ways of thinking that reduce the ability to respond to new information. Initial decisions or judgements are hard to change despite contrary or more complicated matters arising as the interaction continues. Further questioning is influenced by the initial evaluation of what is happening, thus unwittingly reinforcing the original problem-perception. This places the worker in the position of the expert and reduces opportunities for the service user to be properly heard.

SFBT tries to avoid or delay this position by taking what Anderson and Goolishan (1992, p. 29) described as a *not knowing* stance:

> The not knowing position entails a general attitude or stance in which the therapists' actions communicate an abundant, genuine curiosity. That is, the therapists' actions and attitudes express a need to know more about what has been said, rather than convey preconceived opinions and expectations about the client, the problem, or what must be changed. The therapist, therefore, positions himself or herself in such a way as always to be in a state of 'being informed' by the client.

Not-knowing requires asking more questions, rather than thinking that the *truth* has been arrived at. In SFBT, if you think that you have found the answer it is probably wise to start asking further questions, as this may just be your own analysis imposed on the service user. Asking for further detail is important and maintaining a sense of *curiosity* is a key to this approach.

Listening in a solution-focused way is not just about hearing what people have to say about problems, but is also about listening attentively for strengths, exceptions and resilience against the problem. This is not to gloss over the difficulties people face in a superficial manner, but to recognise complexity and that people are often subsumed into discourses of failure that freeze them into helplessness. Complimenting people on their successes is important as this can reinforce strengths that people have undervalued (or have been undervalued for them). Josie complained that her mother had always *done her down* and that everything she did was not good enough for mother's demanding standards. The worker expressed amazement at Josie's patience and skills in managing the unreasonableness of her mother for so long, and wondered how she had been able to do this? Josie was able to describe the strategies and tactics she had employed to contain her mother's behaviour and Josie's own feelings of worthlessness. De Jong and Berg (2002, pp. 35–6) identify three types of compliments: direct, indirect and self-compliments. Direct compliments are strong validations of what people have achieved (You did really well to do that given the circumstances!); indirect compliments imply positives about the service user (So how did you manage to get the four children out of bed, washed, dressed, fed and off to school all on your own?); and self-compliments need to be recognised and validated (I stopped cutting myself because it was getting in the way of college. When did you decide to do something so brave?). Indirect compliments can be useful as they allow the space for service users to reflect on their strengths, rather than direct affirmation from the worker which may reinforce the power differentials between them, giving the worker a rather paternalistic position.

Complimenting is not something that is done simply to make the service user, or the worker, feel good; it is part of the repertoire of tools within the solution-focused approach that has a purpose. Honesty is important here, as service users will be able to see through any forced compliments that do not have genuine meaning. If there is little to compliment, it is not advisable to make it up. The Junction, a Barnardo's service for children with sexual behaviour problems, routinely compliments children on arrival, as the physical act of getting to the office, as well as the emotional strength required to get through the door to talk about difficult matters, demonstrates a level of commitment to dealing with the behaviour. Even when people are mandated or coerced into a service (which is familiar professional territory, be it child protection, offending or mental health for example) they have some choice whether to turn up or not, although their choices may be constrained. Recognising the reality of their situation and being able to see positives in this is worthy of validation.

Problem-free talk

Many service users and professionals come together because of problems so it is understandable that there are assumptions that talk will be about these. Given the caveats previously outlined, SFBT resists the temptation to do this, preferring to focus on talk that is away from the problem and that provides clues for the development of solutions. This has significance not just for the service user but for the worker, as it provides a brake on our tendency, be it professional, personal and cultural, to want to explore the problem, thus inadvertently reinforcing it.

Maintaining problem-free talk is useful in generating the context for solutions to the problem and this can be done from the very first encounter between service user and worker. Counselling practice often encourages an initial *getting to know you* phase where attempts are made to put people at ease through conversations not necessarily related to the issue. SFBT views the whole encounter as productive, so beginning talk can be used to tease out positives, strengths and exceptions, rather than be seen as just a preliminary phase that precedes the *real* work as in other approaches. This is particularly helpful for busy workers who need to utilise their time with service users to the maximum.

Practice Example 4.1

Marie visited Jane, who had been diagnosed with *depression* and there were concerns about her care of the children. Jane appeared to be very unhappy and the home was dark with the curtains drawn even during the day. Jane expressed her misery at the situation and her sense of failure as a parent. Marie heard all this, then asked Jane to tell her about the things that she and her children were good at. Jane was a little perplexed at first, but was able to list a whole series of strengths and achievements of her children, then began to recognise that she was responsible for these.

Marie asked more questions about how Jane had encouraged such positives in her children despite the depression. Jane was able to move to talking about herself and the qualities she had as a parent. Far from being a preliminary *social chit-chat*, the conversation developed from the first as a tool to assist Jane in thinking about how she could deal with the constraining effects of depression using her temporarily hidden strengths. The talk was good humoured as Jane was invited to identify those times when her child had made her proud, including the things that made her laugh. At the end of the session Jane was in a much better frame of mind to work with Marie towards solutions. As Marie left, Jane opened the curtains and let in the light.

Problem-free talk takes as many forms as there are workers and service users and it is not possible to prescribe a formula or form of questions; it depends on the specifics of the situation. Milner and O'Byrne (2004, p. 157) provide the following questions as examples of what might be said:

- I know very little about you apart from what brings you here. What would you feel happy to tell me about yourself?
- What are you interested in?
- What do you enjoy?
- What are you good at?
- [for relatives of the client] What does [client] do that makes you proud of him/her?

Exercise 4.1
- Consider the above questions.
- What other questions might you ask in this manner?
- How would you answer these questions?
- What feelings do these questions generate in you?

How brief is brief therapy?

Interventions within a solution-focused approach assume that it is possible to effect change through purposeful and rigorous application of principles and techniques. However, this is not to say that it is all over in a quick session, although it may well be in some cases. Lipchik (1994) warns of the *rush to be brief*, where workers may pursue the brief aspect of the approach to the detriment of the pace of the service user, driven by their enthusiasm for the model and perhaps by agency requirements for a *quick fix*. Although the work of De Shazer identified that therapeutic interventions did not have to be long-term and intensive to achieve results, the brief element is a relative one and can be thought of as *minimum required intervention*. The model may be brief compared to other models, but one person's brevity is another's long-term therapy.

It may be helpful to consider the first session as potentially the only or last session, as research demonstrates that most change occurs in the initial stages of any therapeutic encounter and that the longer intervention continues the less return there is in terms of impact and change (Cox and Campbell, 2003). There are also problems with dropping-out of longer term therapy, where people vote with their feet when faced with intensive and time consuming meetings which have reducing usefulness for them, plus creating a sense of dependency that is unhelpful for endings (Jordan, 2001). The assumption that the first session can be the last is uncommon in other approaches, but gives a discipline to the work that workers will find helpful in their busy working lives. It raises questions about the nature of professional intervention and the role of the worker. For example, in teaching students I have invited people to consider how long they think that they should be involved in hypothetical case studies. The response tends to be quite vague and the more *problematic* the case the more long-term the perceived intervention. When I then ask them how long they would like social workers to be involved in their own family they are quick to reply that this should be as brief as possible. There are many reasons why intervention should be as short as possible, not least the stigmatising effect of having professional workers intervening, but also moral questions about the role of the state in people's lives.

To impose a structure or timescale that does not fit the individual would be contrary to the respectful approach of SFBT, as well as being *solution-forced* and probably lacking meaning for the person, although it is possible to be optimistic that the intervention can be brief. The following practice techniques will demonstrate how establishing goals allows for achievements to be measured, thus clarifying just how brief the contact needs to be for the individual. Holding on to the notion that intervention does not have to be long-term is important, as many theoretical perspectives tend to assume that problems are entrenched and require long-term, intensive intervention, thus leading to goals and timescales that are impossible to attain within the available resources.

Perkins (2006) describes applying a single two-hour solution-focused session to a large number of children who were referred to a child and adolescent mental health clinic with a range of emotional, behavioural and social problems. She found a remarkable improvement in the children in the follow-up study that led her to conclude that such an approach should be the initial choice for this hard-pressed service, as it is effective, efficient and appreciated by patients. This seems to demonstrate that even where a solution-focused approach is applied in a limited structure it can generate positive change.

Transparency

Solution-focused work lends itself to being entirely open with the service user, as there are no hidden agendas behind the questioning of the worker; they are eliciting information from the person and seeking their meanings rather than analysing it from a professional perspective. In this sense it is relatively easy to explain to people how you work, emphasising that they are the person who knows themselves the best; that everyone has the capacity to change and the strengths to achieve this, and that your role is to work with them to help deal with the problem. This contrasts with some other approaches where the worker is looking for hidden meanings and it can be difficult to explain the theory behind such interventions.

Milner and O'Byrne (2002b, p. 62) give examples of how psychodynamic and systemic family therapy practice is based on assumptions about resistance, transference and unconscious processes that can negatively frame service user actions and would be difficult for service users to accept. Indeed, if service users find the therapy problematic they are viewed as in denial or acting out subconscious dynamics, rather than having a reasonable objection to the basis and form of the intervention. This approach struggles to take service user perspectives as valid in themselves, but as having a *deeper* meaning that only the worker has the key to unlock. Warner (2001) discusses the ways in which therapies based on structural assumptions about the impact of abuse can replicate harmful relationships for women who have experienced childhood sexual trauma, as they tend to pathologise the personal coping strategies of the women by making normative judgements about how women *should* act. How transparency and openness (and partnership and equality) can be possible under these conditions is difficult to imagine, as the service user-worker relationship is inherently unequal.

Exercise 4.2

- Think of a professional intervention you had with someone that had a positive outcome for the service user.
- How did you both agree about the nature of the problem?
- How clear were you with them about your perception of the problem?
- How did you both agree about when the intervention should end?
- How did you plan for the ending?
- In retrospect, could you have ended the work sooner with a reasonable outcome?
- If so, how?

Chapter 5
Beginning a Solution-focused Session: The Problem

Most professional practice requires thought about just what is going to be happening in any encounter with service users. Meeting people for the first time is fraught with potential anxieties and possibilities, and in the context of professional intervention there may be understandable wariness or hostility from the service user about engaging with someone in authority. In thinking about how to go about structuring a session, McMahon's problem solving formula (1996) will be a fairly familiar outline to most workers. The stages are as follows:

- Description of the problem and data collection
- Problem assessment
- Intervention planning
- Intervention
- Evaluation and follow-up

The worker will begin by asking for details about the problem in order to make a professional assessment based on theoretical, research and practice knowledge. Once assessed, the worker and the client can construct a plan informed by the worker's knowledge and implement this; a plan to reduce the effects of the problem. The plan is monitored and any adjustments are made if the intervention is not working. The plan continues until the aims are achieved and the problem has ended. Solution-focused approaches have some similarities and differences to this, and these will become clearer during the rest of this chapter.

De Jong and Berg (2002, pp. 17-18) describe the stages of a solution-building session as:

- Describing the problem
- Developing well-formed goals
- Exploring for exceptions
- End of session feedback
- Evaluating client progress

This sequence uses the process to work towards enhancing solid, achievable solutions to problems; what Jackson and McKergow (2002) describe as building a *platform* on which to reach their *future perfect*.

Introductions

Maintaining a respectful approach to service users is a basic communication skill and *doing respect* takes different forms with different people. This may well be influenced by the circumstances in which the service user finds themselves in contact with professionals and there can be a sense of *deserving* and *undeserving* (or a continuum) service users. Someone who is in hospital and requires assessment about returning home may be viewed as having a right to services that are due to circumstances beyond their control. Someone who has committed an act of violence against another may be seen as less worthy of respect, and of course it becomes immensely complicated when we are faced with the messiness of service users who fall into both extremes some of the time. Assessing the care needs of an older person who has fallen at home may uncover evidence of their violence towards their partner, which throws the binary deserving-undeserving continuum into disarray. This may well impact on the ways in which a worker responds to people. Egan (1998, p. 45) who is influential in social care and counselling practice, says that 'The way you act will tell them a great deal about your attitude'. It is unhelpful to withdraw respect from people if we are concerned to work *with* them in order to deal with the problem and to construct safety.

Professionals engage with people in a variety of settings: in the office; in service user homes; in hospitals; in care establishments and sometimes on the street. The structure of the sessions will be affected by this and some of the more formulaic approaches to SFBT sessions may have to be creatively modified to respond to this. It is usually helpful to introduce each other and to be clear about the role of the worker. Complimenting people about their strength in meeting with you and that this indicates a level of personal commitment can assist the process. With some service users it can be appropriate to begin by asking what they are good at and what makes them laugh, particularly with children and young people, which not only helps to create an easier atmosphere but begins to give clues about strengths.

Explaining to service users that the session will include a lot of what may appear to be strange questions, followed by a space for the worker to think about what has been said, then a time for sharing thoughts about what may be helpful is one way of being transparent. Demystifying what is going to happen helps people to engage, as there can be many assumptions about professional practice that are unhelpful, particularly if the person has had previous intervention based on other models or has been reading newspapers or watching television programmes that are saturated with limited stories about what workers do. Asking what their experience has been previously can elicit what has been useful for them and asking what they hope to achieve from the meeting begins to clarify their expectations (and starts to identify goals), as well as beginning to acknowledge that they have a part to play in this process.

Milner and O'Byrne (2002b, p. 60) are happy to share with service users the notion that as solution-focused therapists they are 'much more interested in where they [service users] are going than where they have been as the past can't be changed', and checking out that this is alright for them. This is not to exclude problem-talk if that is what the service user wants, but sets the scene for the types of questions that are asked. Milner and O'Byrne also suggest that it is helpful to establish that service users do not have to answer questions if they do not want to by giving permission to *pass* on answers. This may seem strange to workers who may feel they need to know certain key information, but consider the example of a young person who is asked if they are still using cannabis. What would pass mean in this situation? Information in SFBT is not treated as something to be found, it is created through the interaction between people and the language that is used leading to opportunities for change.

Being clear about the timescale is important, as a busy worker may have to be pragmatic in the allocation of their resources for individual cases. In situations where there is a more structured environment it may be possible to be very disciplined about the session. Korman (2004, p. 2), working in the field of child and adolescent psychiatry, is able to be clear in saying 'I will ask a lot of questions and after 30–40 minutes I will take a break and go think about what we talked about (talk to the team) and see if I (we) have an idea about what I (we) believe could be helpful'. This sort of resource may not be available to every worker but brings a certain focus to bear that reduces the opportunities for sessions to become long and boring (and counter-productive). Milner and O'Byrne (2002b, p. 61) usually say to service users that the sessions will last about an hour, but that people are free to leave before that if they wish to. They introduce a rule that has developed through their practice which is particularly useful where children are involved, that is that if a child leaves the room then only good things can be said about them in their absence. This avoids parents (and professional carers) taking the opportunity to tell you the catalogue of problems about their behaviour, which the young person is often expecting and may well be listening for behind the door!

Workers operate under certain rules that do not provide for absolute confidentiality. It is important to illustrate what sort of information may have to be shared with others if certain matters came to light, in order that the service user is clear about the consequences of talking. Where it emerges that harm has been or is being done to themselves or others then there needs to be a discussion about what is to be done with this information, although this can be framed in terms of the developing responsibility of the service user. If we are to develop choices then people need to be fully aware of the circumstances in order to make an informed choice about what to talk about. Of course, choice may well be limited, especially for mandated service users, but within this there are possibilities for personal agency.

Describing the problem

It would be unusual for professionals to have to speak with people for whom life was fine and without problems, although of course even the most content and happy of us have some problems at some times in our lives. Social care professionals are expected to talk about difficulties and many service users go into detail about the enormity, frequency and severity of the difficulties they are facing. SFBT would listen attentively to this as respecting what the service user wants to talk about, although De Jong and Berg (2002) warn that this can be a time when the problems may seduce the worker into becoming an expert in diagnosing the matter. Avoiding the professional temptation to make such judgements is a principle of SFBT.

Ensuring that the nature of the problem *for the person* is understood is important to establish, as again there may be a conscious or unconscious drift into worker diagnosis. Asking *how* the problem is a problem for service users is useful in identifying the significance for them, rather than professional assumptions about how people should or may experience a problem. Checking out the meaning of the problem assists in creating workable solutions, as the worker and service user are talking about the same thing!

Milner and O'Byrne (2002b, p. 64) describe a situation where a client had attended counselling because of her eating problems. The counsellor had concentrated on her previous experience of sexual abuse as a probable cause of this behaviour, but the client rejected this as she was concerned about dealing with the immediacy of her eating problems and had no desire to concentrate on previous experiences that could not be changed. A solution-focused approach aided her in constructing strategies for tackling eating, i.e what she wanted to talk about, and the client could return to her past experiences at a time when she wanted to discuss them. Forcing people to talk about the issue chosen by the worker may simply result in withdrawal from the process.

Although talking about the problem will be inevitable, the SFBT worker will use these conversations to destabilise the problem, looking for ways in which the problem was less or resisted. An SFBT approach would move away from problem-talk as soon as is practicable, and De Jong and Berg (2002, p. 59) say that this is when the service user has had the chance to say enough to be heard, suggesting that this takes about 10-15 minutes. Practice in SFBT varies, with some workers moving quickly to solutions, although this runs the danger previously raised about being *solution-forced*.

Pre-session change

If the SFBT worker is not an expert in the diagnostic sense, then asking the service user what has changed in the period between referral and meeting is important, as life is not static and *change is always happening*. This is different from many therapeutic approaches which consider the engine of change to be the relationship between therapist and service user. SFBT recognises that sometimes problems come and go, as do solutions, so inviting people to describe what is different since the problem was identified begins to explore possible solutions. Where there are changes for the better the worker will ask the person how this happened, with an emphasis on what they did to achieve this change. Validating these changes, however small, can encourage further engagement in the process. With children, it may be that someone has treated them in a certain way that has been helpful, so this enables clues about what works for the child. Assuming that people or circumstances do not change before the worker arrives on the scene can lead to confusion and irrelevant conversations. Sometimes, the very act of knowing that you have to see a professional can effect change, perhaps through knowing that you need to clean the house to a required standard or ensure that your children attend school or that you may go to prison if you do not mend your ways. Checking this out will assist in thinking about how this change can be sustained and in SFBT, *if it works do more of it*.

There is research evidence that pre-session change occurs regularly, for example Allgood *et al.* (1995) found that 30 per cent of 200 clients seeking therapy had reported pre-therapeutic improvement and Johnson *et al.* (1998) found that those people who reported such change were four times more likely to complete therapy than those who did not. Clearly identifying and validating pre-session change can have a significant impact on the success of interventions. The change itself is useful, but it is also a source of ideas for developing future strategies.

Pre-suppositional questions are useful here; questions that are leading in that they are communicating a pre-existing belief or expectation. Leading questions are often seen as anathema in interviewing practice, but if done sensitively and purposefully they can be helpful (O'Hanlon and Weiner-Davies, 1988). Within the language games that we operate no question is neutral and will always have some contested meaning. Asking service users when they have tried to deal with the problem, rather than if they have, requires them to think about the positive steps they may have already taken.

De Shazer (1988) and Berg and Miller (1992) used their experiences at the Brief Family Therapy Centre to develop a typology of service users to assist in thinking about what may be specifically helpful, given the different ways in which people engage with therapeutic services. The types are: *Customer*; *Complainant* and *Visitor*. The willingness and motivation of people to change is inevitably affected by the context in which they approach or are sent to services, and workers can find themselves engaging with a range of people with widely different expectations. The following types are not to be seen as personality traits or fixed in any way; they are ways of describing relationships rather than a category of person. They cannot be absolutely linked to the reasons for referral, and as De Jong and Berg (2002, p. 60) say, 'Although we have found it more likely that we will establish customer-type relationships with so-called voluntary clients than with involuntary clients, we cannot predict what would happen in any particular case.'

Customer

This can be seen as the most straightforward of relationships, where the service user and the worker jointly agree on the problem and solutions based on the willingness of the service user to engage with the service. Often this relationship is one where the service user has decided that they need help and are willing to accept this, already having the motivation to deal with the problem. They have ideas for solutions which provide the basis for the development of clear goals.

Complainant

This type of relationship is where the problem can be identified but the service user cannot see how they can play a part in developing a solution. The problem and solutions are located elsewhere, often in the behaviour of another person or the context in which the problem exists. Often the person wants the worker to change the behaviour of someone else, rather than seeing themselves as having some part to play in this. A feeling of powerlessness can pervade these sessions and there is a tendency to expect the worker to *sort the other person out*. A parent who is having difficulties with the behaviour of their child or couples who are struggling with each other are frequent cases of this type. They may wish for advice on how to sort the other person out themselves, placing the worker in the position of an expert, imparting knowledge that can assist them.

SFBT would see this handing over of responsibility as problematic, as it will probably not be the most effective local way of dealing with the problem. Developing responsibility is important, but there is no need to do what Egan (1994, p. 161) suggested, which is challenging clients' 'failure to own problems', as this emphasises deficit. It is more constructive to hear what people's perceptions are and to try to move from problem-talk to solution-talk. A father was frustrated by his son's poor behaviour and wanted the Youth Offending Team worker to tell the son that unless he changed his ways he would go into care. The worker listened to what the father had to say and acknowledged that the father cared for his son very much and wanted the best for him. The worker asked questions about when the son's behaviour had been better and how the father had managed to assist his son in behaving well. The father was able to think of times when they had been doing things together that seemed to be less problematic, and that he had successfully dealt with some problem behaviour previously by imposing a sensible sanction. The worker also asked if the father could think of things that his son would be saying about him if the behaviour had changed. The father was able to imagine that his son was saying that he had spent more time with him and done several activities that they had previously enjoyed together, as well as talking more about the loss of his mother which they had not done for a long time. The worker and the father were able to consider a strategy to help the son behave less badly.

Milner and O'Byrne (2004, p.166) give an excellent example of how to respond to a situation where a teacher, who is in the hugely problematic circumstance of trying to keep order in a class of 35 children, is having difficulties with one boy who is disruptive. Often the teacher, who has the needs of the whole class to consider, wants the child to change and can only see them as a problem. A solution-focused approach assumes that the problem is not always there nor takes the same form. They ask teachers to help in the development of a solution through undertaking tasks such as:

> . . . by listing, in detail, those times when he/she is or was doing better in class. We use our own 'report card' to facilitate this process. This resembles an ordinary school report card but is two-sided. One side asks the teacher to report on what the pupil has done right in each lesson, and the other asks them to report what the pupil has done wrong. However, there is a rider to the 'wrong' side which says 'do not write anything on this side of the card until you have written something on the other side'. We find that even the most truculent pupil will turn up for lessons, and behave, for the sheer pleasure of watching a disliked teacher write something good about them.

Once the teacher can recognise that there are times when the behaviour is better, this allows for exploration of what makes it better, including the actions of the teacher, and how more of this can be done.

Visitor

This type of relationship applies in many cases where the person has no choice but to visit or be visited by the professional. Involuntary, mandated or limited-choice service users abound in many professional contexts and this relationship will be familiar to many readers. The service user does not see a problem; it has been defined by someone else and is seen as their issue. So people who have been sent by the courts, or because of child protection concerns or due to concerns that they may not be coping in the community, may all be reluctant to accept that there is anything to work on. This is a perfectly reasonable position to take, given the strength of emotion generated by being coerced into doing something that locates the blame in you. This reluctance to engage merely reflects the situation the person finds themselves in, where others are making decisions about what they need to do, leading to what De Jong and Berg (2002, p. 68) describe as a natural response of 'defiance, resistance and a desire to subvert others' attempts at control'. Of course, people who will not do what you want them to, or what you think is in their best interests, run the risk of being labelled as uncooperative, in denial, having Oppositional Defiance Disorder, or just plain difficult. It is perhaps more helpful, and also generates a patient attitude, to think of this as not *yet* having found a way of working that is right for the person. Indeed, De Shazer (1991) reframes this apparent *lack* of cooperation as a *different* way of cooperating, as service users are telling the practitioner, through their behaviour, that the current practice is not working for them. This reminds us that *if it ain't working, do something different*, rather than pursue an approach that is inappropriate.

Visitors can be invited to ponder on how much of the problem that has been identified by others is their responsibility, in a non-blaming way that allows some dignity. Jacob (2001, p. 30) describes a young woman who was forced to come to therapy by her mother, who was worried about her daughter's eating problems. The young woman was very resistant to engaging and made the eating problem simply an anxiety of her mother's concern. She was invited to use a scale of 1 to 10 (more of which later in Chapter 8) about her likelihood of eating a large meal, where 1 is 'There's a snowball's chance in Hell' and 10 is 'You'd eat fish and chips and pudding for definite?' Similarly, a boy who had been offending and could not see a problem because all his mates were doing it was asked 'If 1 is no chance at all, and 10 is absolutely certain, what chance is there that your current behaviour will land you in jail?' Both scales enabled the people to take some appropriate responsibility for their behaviour, as people rarely give themselves a 1 or a 10, thus opening opportunities for thinking about the problem for *them*, rather than for *others*.

Where there is a complete refusal to acknowledge that the behaviour is problematic then it is still possible to pursue questions to open up this for self-investigation. Consider the following. Jane's aggressive behaviour at home and school had led to despair in both places. She refused to see any difficulties with this, saying that she was expressing her feelings and that if people didn't like it then it was their problem and she saw no reason to change. It had indeed become their problem, as there was a list of verbal and physical assaults peppered with racist invective. Jane was asked to amplify her thinking by questions such as 'How has this behaviour helped you in your life? When has it helped you to get on with your family? How has it helped you to make friends at school? On a scale of 1 to 10, where 1 is the Devil and 10 is an Angel, where would you place yourself? Where would your parents, teachers or friends place you?' Further questions were asked about other people's perceptions of her behaviour, for example 'If I was to ask your friends what they like about your behaviour, what would they say? What would your brother and sister say about your behaviour? What sort of behaviour does your mother like? When have you behaved in that way?' Maintaining a calm and puzzled approach focused on exploring the meaning of the behaviour for Jane was crucial to developing understanding and allowing some space for change.

De Jong and Berg (2002, pp. 70–71) provide helpful guidelines for visitor relationships where there may be reluctance to engage:

- Assume the client has good reason to think and act as he or she does
- Suspend your judgement and agree with the client's perceptions that stand behind his or her cautious, protective posture
- Be sure to ask for the client's perception of what is in his or her best interest, that is, ask what the client might want. Accept the client's answer. (Implicit in asking someone a question is your willingness to accept that person's opinion)
- Listen for and reflect the client's use of language, instead of trying to paraphrase the client's words into your way of speaking

In some cases there may be repeated and fruitless attempts to develop change, as SFBT is not the answer for everyone's problems all of the time, and there may be the need for enforcement action to be taken where safety is undeveloped.

Exercise 5.1

- Remember the last time a service user came to you with a label (difficult; uncommunicative; bully; victim; *etc.*)
- How did you avoid seeing their label as the whole person?
- How did you find out about the times when they were not their label?
- How did you find out about their understanding of their label?

Chapter 6
Developing Goals: The Miracle Question

Problem-talk tends to remain in the past or the present, without much focus on what people need to do to move forward. Aphorisms such as 'you need to understand the past to move on' are commonplace, but there is little evidence that this is the case and they reflect more of a cultural expectation than any absolute key to a problem-free future. SFBT is interested in goals; what people want in order to create a strategy for getting there. Imagining what would be different when you have a problem-free life (if you like, the destination), allows then for consideration of how you might get there (the means of transport). This future-oriented approach turns the past-orientation of other methods on its head, seeking answers in the imagined future rather than the past, which of course is also imagined through the lens of hindsight and insight.

SFBT is interested in assisting people to identify their goals at an early stage in any encounter and, following Wittgenstein, there is an assumption that when people talk about a problem they already have the seeds of a solution within this. To describe a problem is to implicitly describe what life without the problem would look like. If someone's problem is their use of drugs, then the preferred problem-free life is one without using drugs. The person will know when they have dealt with the problem when it is no longer a problem, therefore this becomes measurable. Talking about goals does not avoid the problem, as when we discuss a goal there is an acknowledgement that it exists in relation to the problem. Goals are created to eradicate the problem. In working with 'John', a boy who had offended, he was invited to consider what his goals were for an offending-free future. He was able to describe many personal and social events that would be happening, most of which seemed to have no direct link with the behaviour (going out with friends; having a girlfriend; working in a decent job; having a car; getting on better with his parents). However, they were goals that he felt would be present when he was *not* offending, thus maintaining the link and still retaining a sense of responsibility for changing his behaviour. Saleeby (1994, p. 357) describes the importance of imagining goals thus: 'Only when people start creating scenarios of possibility do they move in directions more satisfying to them, and problems become lost or much less influential.'

Goal formation can begin with early introductions, and solution-focused practitioners often structure initial questions to encourage this. The Brief Therapy Practice (www.brieftherapy.org.uk) uses 'What is your best hope from this session?' allowing the person to consider their immediate goals and giving some ideas for achieving these. Quite often people may feel that major change is desired, but achieving this can be unimaginable at this stage in the process. If someone says that they want all their problems sorted out and have a perfect life, they may well feel that the task is too enormous and become daunted at the prospect of achieving this. SFBT practitioners value the small and the achievable as building blocks for further steps, so asking people what small thing (feelings, actions or thoughts) would be different for the session to have been useful can be more imaginable. Asking service users what would be different in their lives, however small, for the session to have been useful for them can also provide clues for goals and what service users want. Without some sense of what they want it is difficult to ask the right questions to assist them in getting there; the space created by a lack of service user goals can easily be filled by the worker's agenda which would not be helpful in creating meaningful change. Another useful way of encouraging goal-formation is to ask 'What would you need to be doing to no longer have to see me?' which, with mandated service users, acknowledges that choice is restrained.

Goals need to be important to the service user, which may conflict with some professional roles where there are specific concerns that require addressing. However, most service users have problems that are creating difficulties for them or others, and are aware of the purpose of the encounter with workers. Asking service users what they want is usually seen within the context of the referral rather than some general conversation amongst friends. Initial goals may be vague or general, and the worker can ask further questions for clarification. If someone who presents with depression says that they want to have *good self-esteem*, then the worker can ask gentle questions about how they would know when they had good self-esteem or what would they be doing differently when they had good self-esteem? This is particularly helpful when faced with people who want an improvement in feelings, as these can be difficult to quantify, and asking for clarity about what sort of actions or behaviours are associated with feeling better gives both the service user and the worker a more tangible picture of the desirable feelings. This situation can be assisted by using the perceptions of significant others to look at what would be happening when things are better, as some people may be puzzled by the idea of what they would be doing without the problem.

Where problems are seen to be all-encompassing, it is helpful to try to de-stabilise this by breaking down the problems to their time and place, as most problems do not happen everywhere all the time, although it may feel like it. For example, a student presented as upset and on the verge of leaving her studies because she was 'completely disorganised, I can't get a grip on anything and can't get my assignments in on time'. She was asked what part of her disorganisation she wanted to work on, choosing which was the most important for her at the moment. She decided to work on organising her time for her studies and let the other disorganised parts of her life carry on, as she had bumped along reasonably well up to that point. It was decided that the part of the problem that caused her most anxiety, and had the severe consequences of her failing the course, needed attention, so this became the goal. Of course, this had the effect of unsettling her description of the problem as total, which she was able to use to tackle those other parts of her life that could do with some attention, in her own time and having recognised her own resources.

In SFBT, goals that are about the *absence of something undesirable* are seen as a starting point for developing goals that are about the *presence of something desirable.* Because people present with problems they quite understandably may talk about a goal being a life without the problem; that the problem will have gone. However, this leaves rather a gap about what will replace it. As Miller (1997, p. 75) says: 'Change will not be sustained if a void is not filled with something new. Stories that only emphasise giving up troublesome behaviours actually direct clients' attention to that which they are supposed to avoid.'

If a parent facing concerns about the care of their child says that they will work towards a future where social services are not in their lives (*off my back!*), then this is a laudable intention but requires some thought about what will be different when this happens. Asking questions about what will be happening if this is the case opens up a more constructive dialogue about the presence of actions that are needed to remove social workers from the family. So it may be that the parent will be getting on better with her children, they will be going to school on time; they will be dressed and breakfasted and she will be feeling much better about her parenting skills. This becomes a goal that is about actions that have meaning for her as well as addressing the concerns of professionals. In working with boys who have offended, asking them what they hope for the future (goals) can often lead to vague commitments to stop getting into bother. This can be explored by asking them what they will be doing differently when they have stopped. How will their parents know they have stopped, what will they be doing to show people, including me as their supervisor, that they have stopped? This begins to tease out some of the activities they are interested in and provides clues about their local circumstances and helpful relationships. They may well say that they will have stopped offending but will be playing football, helping around the house, going out with safe mates, getting to college on time, not doing as much cannabis and saying no to offers to get into further bother. SFBT practitioners will seek further information about what people will be doing differently by gently probing with 'and what else?' until there is a fairly comprehensive picture emerging of measurable and achievable goals.

Developing realistic and measurable goals is a key element of SFBT, as this allows the service user to be clear about what they can achieve and when they can achieve this. If it is clear, then it can be measured and held to account. If service users have goals that are unrealistic, then it is helpful to assist them in thinking about how these goals can be broken down into more achievable parts, as unrealistic goals will lead to a sense of failure and de-skilling.

Practice Example 6.1

A parent who was deeply concerned about the behaviour of their teenage son had a vision of the future where he would be perfect; happy, smiling, helping, doing well at school, dressing well and talking openly with her. Going from fairly expected teenage behaviour (pushing boundaries, sleeping late, struggling to communicate with his parents, making the wrong friends, scrapes with the law) to the best child ever was clearly a large imagined step, and one that seemed a good aspiration, if a little unrealistic. The worker expressed their agreement that this would be a great outcome, but wondered how realistic the parent felt that this was, and how she would know if her son had begun to make steps towards this goal? The parent was able to laugh that perhaps she was expecting too much too soon, and that she would know he was on the road to this ideal when he would get out of bed when she asked him first time in the morning. This was a goal that was much more achievable and one that was worked on, with some success. It also led to discussions about what she could do differently to help him get out of bed in the morning, based on tactics that she had previously tried that had worked, thus shifting the focus of change away just from her son and into a collaborative effort.

Goals need to be legal and moral and if they are a danger to the person or others then action may have to be taken to ensure safety. If a young person says that they ideally want to be a successful drug dealer, earning lots of money, driving flash cars and having an exploitative sexual life, it would be highly irresponsible to assist him in seeking ways to achieve his goal. Of course, some aspects are legal and others less so, and the image is very culturally attractive. Exploring different ways of achieving the legal elements of the goal may be helpful here. Some goals may appear to be delusional, particularly where people have mental health problems, but there is practice experience that demonstrates that these can still be worked with constructively. Hawkes (2003) gives good examples of how people who have been diagnosed with mental illnesses, particularly psychosis, are routinely dismissed as not having the capacity to make rational decisions or choices, therefore becoming subjected to interventions that reduce opportunities for collaborative work. He gives the example of someone hearing voices who has a goal of becoming the next England football manager, which may, on the face of it, seem part of a complex of irrational belief systems. Hawkes makes the point that this diagnosis is irrelevant to a great extent, as the steps needed to become the England manager require concrete actions about going to football training, taking his medication to assist him to worry less, and making his bed to get on better with his mother, all actions that are helpful for him generally and over which he can have some control.

The miracle question

One of the key techniques within SFBT for assisting in the creation of goals and a problem-free future is the *miracle question*. This device has developed from therapeutic approaches that have posed hypothetical questions and there have been variations of this model for some time. Ansbacher and Ansbacher (1998) describe the use of the *magic wand* question, where someone will be asked 'If I had a Magic Wand or pill that would eliminate your symptom immediately, what would be different in your life?' Erickson and Rossi (1980) used a *crystal ball* technique that allowed people to look into the future to see a life free of problems. Berg (1994) and De Shazer (1988) introduced their own version of hypothetical solution-oriented questions in the form of the miracle question. This can take several forms in the way that it is expressed, to a certain extent depending on the service user and the context, but De Shazer (1988, p. 5) provides a comprehensive statement of what it should look like:

> Now, I want to ask you a strange question. **Suppose** that while you are sleeping tonight and the entire house is quiet, a **miracle** happens. The miracle is that **the problem which brought you here is solved**. However, because you are sleeping, you don't know that **the miracle has happened**. So, when you wake up tomorrow morning, **what will be different** that will tell you that a miracle has happened and the problem which brought you here is solved? (original emphasis)

This can be simplified to:

> If the problem disappeared overnight, by magic, what would your next day be like? (Sharry *et al.*, 2003, p. 30)

The key elements of the miracle question are that, because it is a miracle, it invites people to imagine limitless possibilities for their lives to enable them to identify what changes they would want to achieve. It is also future-oriented, moving away from rumination on past and present problems to thinking about what a problem-free life would look like. The question invites people to consider the actions and behaviours that would be happening when their problems have disappeared, which allows for more detail to be developed and a richer picture to emerge. Initially, people may describe more of a *photograph* of the future and the worker can assist them in developing a *video* of the ways in which this will be happening. The miracle question is used to generate goals that can then be worked towards and those goals are set by the person, rather than imposed assumptions by the worker.

The miracle question can elicit puzzlement and laughter from service users, who are generally unused to being asked about their dreams. Some practitioners prefer to pose the question in dramatic terms, using a range of strategies to provide the maximum impact. De Jong and Berg (2003, p. 86) provide the following guidelines for asking the question:

- Speak slowly and gently, in a soft voice, to give your client time to shift from a problem focus to a solution focus
- Mark the beginning of the solution-building process clearly and dramatically by introducing the miracle question as unusual or strange
- Use frequent pauses, allowing the client time to absorb the question and process his or her experiences through its different parts
- Since the question asks for a description of the future, use future-directed words: What *would* be different? What *will* be the signs of the miracle?
- When probing and asking follow-up questions, frequently repeat the phrase 'a miracle happens and the problem that brought you here is solved', in order to reinforce the transition to solution talk
- When clients lapse back into problem talk, gently refocus their attention on what will be different in their lives when the miracle happens

Although this may appear to be quite formulaic, some practitioners find that the shortened version is not as effective in encouraging people to think about their future. It may be that the drama of asking in a particular way provides the environment and gives permission for people to enter into this speculation. If people answer that they do not know, it can be helpful to wait and give them space to think further. Silences in conversations are often filled unnecessarily; give the service user time to think and view the *don't know* as a temporary state of being rather than an absolute. They may not know an answer at that precise time, but after thinking further can often provide some suitable answers.

The miracle scenario can then be made richer by follow-up questions, always striving for detail. If someone says that they will have *won the lottery*, then you can ask what will be different when they have won? What sort of things would they be doing differently? How would other people notice they had won the lottery? Which of these things could be done before the cheque comes? If a young person says that *the police would be off his back*, then he could be asked what he would be doing differently when the police are not after him? What would his parents notice about him? A man who has been domestically violent may say that he and his partner will be *getting on and communicating better without arguing* can be asked what he would be doing differently when this is happening, and how would his partner and children know that things were different? What does getting on and communicating better look like?

Follow-up questions are designed to assist in the creation of concrete behavioural goals in which the service user plays a part. They can be reinforced through reference to interactions with significant others, which helps to make the scenario more realistic and not simply about their perceptions of the solution, by inviting them to consider the views of people who are important in their lives. The questions also provide the opportunity to identify small steps towards the goal, as by asking 'What is the first thing that they or others would notice is different?'

is usually the basis of an achievable action. When asked what would be the first thing her daughter would notice about her behaviour if the miracle had happened, a mother who had been having problems in their relationship was able to say that she would be smiling more and talking calmly to her child. This presented an opportunity to think about how she could achieve this. The use of *what else?* is helpful here to allow further detail that is local to the person, and therefore potentially more meaningful. The imagined miracle may be an aspiration, but it provides the material for thinking about how to get there, or even part of the way.

This technique does not engage directly with the problem as it is about solutions, so talking about the causes and nature of the problem, including how to deal with it, is avoided, and is linked to the notion that understanding or talking about the problem is not a pre-requisite for developing solutions. The process is about hope and positive outcomes, which provide a richer source of ideas for achieving a problem-free life and help people to talk themselves into change and competencies. The question avoids any blaming tendencies as it is difficult to be blamed for the future, but very easy to be pilloried for the past, either by yourself or others. Occasionally people may (quite reasonably) consider that miracles are a figment of the imagination and do not happen in the real world. Where the use of the word miracle is unhelpful, it is possible to invite people to describe a time in the future when the problem has vanished or is less of a problem-what would be happening if this was the case? And of course words such as magic, magic wand and miracle have been used by adults in their grooming of children in cases of sexual abuse, so care needs to be taken when working with children who may have experienced this and thus other forms of words should be used.

Asking the miracle question can be seen to be rather technical by imposing a structure onto people. However, it elicits answers that are unique to that person and it is useful to remember that no matter how many times you use it, it will be the first time that person has considered it. Their responses and the follow-up questions lead to uncharted territory that is made clearer through detail questions, such as outlined above. A genuine curiosity and interest in what people have to say is extremely important, no matter how unlikely or how contrary to your understanding of the world these answers or responses may at first appear.

This technique assists in developing concrete, behavioural and measurable goals through the perspective of the person. Having goals to aim for provides the basis for change; without them it is hard to see how people can effect the sometimes necessary shift in their behaviour and situation that is required.

Berg and Reuss (1998) have found that there are some service users who struggle with the miracle question and find a *nightmare question* more helpful, as they have a fairly bleak view of the world. This poses the miracle question in reverse, as in the following example:

> Suppose that when you go to bed tonight . . . a nightmare occurs. In this nightmare all the problems that brought you here suddenly get as bad as they can possibly get . . . But this nightmare comes true. What would you notice tomorrow that would let you know you were living a nightmare life?

The follow-up questions will look for details about what will be happening, who will be affected and how this might have been prevented or done differently. It opens the possibility that things are not as bad as they could be and invites consideration of what is happening currently that makes the problems less than the nightmare scenario.

Practice Example 6.2

A boy who was using hard drugs was able to imagine that he would be alone in a derelict building, injecting heroin, ill, overdosing and without any friends or family that were supporting him. We were able to talk about what other people would be thinking about him; who would be concerned about his situation; what he could have done differently to prevent this happening; who could have helped him to avoid this future and how far he thought he was along the road to this future. This allowed for further thinking about the personal strengths and supports that he currently had, and could utilise, to avoid such a dreadful outcome.

Learning from the future

SFBT practitioners have found it useful to use lessons from an imagined good future with service users, as these will be located within the experience and desires of the person. Cappaccione (1979) developed the idea of a *letter from the future* where someone is invited to think about having achieved their goals in life perhaps ten years ahead. Imagining that they are their future successful self, they are asked to think about what the goal is like and how they managed to achieve it, being as detailed as possible and including all the ways in which they successfully dealt with the obstacles along the road to a preferred future. The letter is one of encouragement to the present self, pointing out all their qualities that were used to get to that position, including how other people helped as well. It includes a description of all the benefits of the successful future and the reasons why it is so important to try and reach it.

This particular approach has been useful across a range of service users and is illustrated here in work with a boy who had severe learning and behavioural difficulties. His behaviour was of concern, together with a multitude of other problems, and it had been hard to find any approach that he found useful. He was invited to write a letter from his future, since his writing was really good, where he was 25 years old and had achieved all his goals. He was able to produce a detailed scenario of having a house, a girlfriend who he was marrying, two dogs, a car, a steady job and had just come back from a holiday in Spain. He was getting on well with his girlfriend and they were in love. He enjoyed describing this in increasing detail, all about the ways in which his life was perfect. He was then able to think about how he had got there and wrote to himself about the things he had had to do along the way, which were all relevant to his current situation. He had to go to college, be respectful to girls so that he could have a girlfriend, behave well and stay out of trouble with the police and sort out difficulties with his parents. This formed the basis of more discussions about how he was going to do these things and what were immediately achievable. Rather than being viewed as impulsive, having a short attention-span and a lack of ability to sustain plans, he had found a way to articulate what he wanted and to develop plans for how to get there.

Milner and O'Byrne (2002b) have found that using a *back to the future* exercise is also helpful, where the person is invited to imagine that they are in a car that can fly into a successful future to see what they are doing. They are asked to spy on themselves to see just what is happening in this future and to describe in detail what they find. Then the future self sees the present self and invites them to discuss how they managed to achieve this, providing helpful hints about what it took to get there. This scenario has been productive for people of all ages, although it helps if they have seen the film. Disbelief can be suspended as it is when we watch a movie and this can be fun to do.

Durrant (1993) discusses the use of language that implies certainty in the future; language that assumes that change is achievable and will have happened. Thus talking about the future as problem-free implies that this can be made to happen and that people have the capacity to make these changes. So asking 'When the problem is solved what *will* you be doing?' is an optimistic, competency-based question that opens up the possibility of change and agency.

Exercise 6.1

As a worker you know that you struggle to complete the required agency forms on time. This causes you anxiety, especially when you and your supervisor are under pressure due to frequent inspections. Imagine that tonight you go home, have dinner and relax, then go to bed as usual. During the night something miraculous happens, and the problems you have in completing the forms disappear completely. Because you are asleep you do not know that this is the case.

- When you go to work in the morning, what will be the first thing you notice that will tell you that the miracle has happened?
- What will your colleagues notice that is different?
- What will your supervisor notice that is different?
- What will you be doing differently?

Chapter 7
Exceptions, Strengths and Successes: Scaling Questions

Having established what goals the person wants to achieve, the next step is to find a way to get to them. SFBT is interested in utilising the person's local knowledge to construct their most effective route towards a problem-free future, based on the assumption that they are the expert in their life and already have the wherewithal to do this. This, of course, is different from most approaches that presume that the person lacks some skill or ability, requiring input to correct, develop or enhance various aspects of their personality with the direction of the worker. As problems are not total, absolute or fixed, although they may appear so, SFBT is interested in those times when the problem was less or not happening. De Shazer (1985) described *exceptions* as those times when the problem might reasonably have been expected to occur but somehow did not. Seeking and acknowledging exceptions is a key element of SFBT, with the purpose of pondering on how these times may assist in developing strategies to deal with the problem.

Practice Example 7.1

Sharon was angry that her teenage son refused to do anything she asked of him and was also miserable, grumpy and a general pain. She could accept that this was a familiar teenage story, but was incandescent that she had struggled to provide a good home for him by herself and that he now behaved in this way *just like his rubbish father*. She was asked whether there were any times recently when he had not been grumpy, and she was able to think of a day the previous week when he had been helpful to his grandmother. This began to open up the possibility that her son could be *good* and we were able to think about what was happening when he was doing this and how she could encourage him to do more of it. If Sharon had been unable to find anything good to say, it would have been possible to ask her if the grandmother would say that he had been less of a pain at any time, thus inviting another perspective.

When identifying exceptions it is important to ask for more detail, which is why recent examples are helpful as they tend to be fresh in the memory. The detail of exceptions provides clues for what things are like when they are working well, interrogating the good times to understand how they function. This is different from the problem-focused approaches outlined earlier, which tend to be interested in the nature, content and processes of the problem-times. In talking with a boy who had offended, it was clear that his offending formed only a small percentage of his overall behaviour. There was much more of his time that was spent *not* offending and doing other things than getting into bother. These times were of interest to the SFBT worker, and she sought detail about them, asking him what was happening; what he was doing instead; who was with him; how often this happened and where he was when he was not offending. He identified that he was at school; with non-offending mates; at the youth centre; at home; getting on with his mother; occupied doing things and not bored; playing football and helping his mother doing chores. This allowed for recognition of his ability to behave well (sometimes) and to think about what encouraged him to stay out of trouble.

Exceptions to problems tend to be overlooked, so finding them can be difficult and they need reinforcing when they appear. By asking further detailed questions and including compliments this can strengthen the acceptance of skills and competencies.

Practice Example 7.2

Jane had been seen to be shouting loudly at her small children and becoming frustrated and angry with them, causing people concern about her parenting capacity. When asked about those times when she would usually have shouted but did not, she was able to think of a recent occasion in the supermarket when she had spoken calmly to her misbehaving children because she did not want to be embarrassed in public. She was asked *how did you do that?* and was able to describe taking a deep breath and thinking of some of the nice times she had had with the children. This gave clues for Jane to think about how she could use the same or similar techniques in the future, providing her with ways of dealing with her children that enhanced her existing skills and developed her personal agency. Rather than imposing a set of externally constructed parenting skills, she was able to recognise and draw on her personal experience to plot her own course to deal with the problem, using the exceptions to follow her easiest path to a problem-free future (Dolan, 1991).

The *how do you do exceptions* question is a useful one as it requires people to think about their successful actions and to recognise that they do have some control over circumstances. Earlier in this section I raised the significance of pre-session change in SFBT as a source of ideas for working forward. Exception questions lend themselves well to identifying any changes, such as: 'Since you were referred to this service, have there been any times when the problem has been less of a problem?'; 'What have been your best times since the referral?'; 'What were you doing differently when they were good?' or 'When have you thought you have made some small step towards reaching your goal?' De Shazer

(1993, p. 16) says that noticing differences is important in constructing solutions, as '. . . difference opens up the possibility of new meanings, [and] behaviours . . . developing'.

Exceptions can be seen as *deliberate*, where someone can see that their different actions were able to effect change in the usually problematic situation, or *random*, where the person cannot account for the difference (De Jong and Berg, 2002, p. 105). If someone is asked how they did that exception or how it happened, they may well answer that they do not know. Being faced with *I don't know* will be a common experience for many workers asking service users for explanations about their behaviour, but this can simply be a response to the way in which the question has been posed. SFBT tends to avoid asking people why they have done something or why it has happened, as the question has many answers and as *things just happen* it is uninterested in causality. Being asked *why?* can generate feelings of blame, introspection and speculation, focused on the problem. It is much less threatening to ask questions that begin with *how?*, *when?*, *where?*, *who?* and *what?*, as these invite descriptions rather than cause-finding. As Wittgenstein (1963, p. 109) says 'We must do away with all explanation, and description alone must take its place' in order to be clearer about what is happening.

When faced with *I don't know* answers it may be helpful to think of this as a temporary phenomenon, assuming that the service user does not yet know or is not yet able to articulate what has happened. Milner and O'Byrne (2002b, p. 43) provide some ideas based on their extensive practice for responding to this and aiding the person to think further about it:

- No reaction, other than a puzzled expression (after all, it is the client's turn to speak)
- Maybe you know and don't know at the same time-that's hard to say . . .
- Acknowledge they 'don't know' and wait, pretending that's not the answer
- I always think that when people do things they must have some idea of how to do it . . .
- Of course you don't know yet; so what do you think?
- Okay, so what do you think your mum/best pal would know?
- Suppose you did know, what might the answer be?
- Perhaps I have not asked the question in a helpful way-how could I ask it better?
- [for small children] Oh I see. It's a secret. Okay.
- Perhaps you might like to study what happens next time and see if you can spot how you do it?

The use of verbal and non-verbal cues to encourage people to think further requires a certain approach by the worker based on genuine curiosity and respecting where people may be at that point. Where people are crushed by their circumstances into believing that they have no part to play in change (are disempowered), then the worker has a responsibility to gently tease out those subordinated times when things were not as problematic and amplify what exactly was going right.

Scaling questions

Exceptions allow for the recognition of strengths that people have in successfully dealing with a problem and begin to generate hope in an otherwise bleak landscape. Every exception has the potential to demonstrate strengths and this can be clarified through detail questions. One of the common techniques of SFBT is that of *scaling questions*, where people are invited to rate their perceptions of the problem and their capacities, confidence and willingness to deal with the situation. The technique is simple and has been found to be accessible to a wide range of people, even where intellectual and educational ability is limited (Greene and Kondrat, 2006). A scale of 0 to 10 is generally used and scaling questions can be used at several points in the process of an interview. They can be used to think about 'self-esteem, pre-session change, client self-confidence, investment in change, willingness to work hard to bring about desired changes, prioritising of problems to be solved, perception of hopefulness, and evaluation of progress' (Berg, 1994, pp. 102–103). The scale is structured so that the numbers are all pointing towards solutions, as even a 1 is a move forward from 0. Of course, these scales are not an absolute or *scientific* measure; they are the product of the subjective experience of the person and do not have any meaning outside what the person gives them. This is unlike some psychometric measures that claim to have a true numeric value of a thought, feeling or event. Scales in SFBT provide a relative value for the person and the worker, as if it is at 8 then this is better than 7, much better than 4, and getting towards 10.

Scales assist in talking in more concrete terms about things that can be hard to describe.

Exercise 7.1

- Consider the last piece of work you undertook with a service user.
- On a scale of 0–10, where 0 is the worst work you could have done, and 10 is the very best, where would you rate this piece of work?
- What would you have been doing differently if you had been able to rate it at the next highest number?
- How would the service user have known that you were doing it at the higher number?
- How would your supervisor have known that you were doing it at the higher number?
- What will you be doing differently to achieve the higher number next time?

Scales allow for comparisons, and it is rare, but not unheard of, as we will see later, for people to rate themselves as 0 or 10. The follow-up questions are also oriented towards the future and provide helpful hints for progress.

Scaling is often introduced into contacts with service users at an early stage, including trying to identify and amplify pre-session change. For example, a service user can be asked 'If 0 is the worst the problem can be, and 10 is the complete absence of the problem, where would you rate the problem at the moment?' Whatever people reply, this allows the service user to begin to talk about their understanding of the problem and to share this perception with you, providing opportunities for detail conversations. Consider how different this question is from asking 'Things were bad when you were asked to see me, how bad are they now?' The scale provides a convenient structure on which to begin to make some sense of the situation, whereas the latter question is much more open-ended and less focused, inviting a wide-ranging exploration. The scale provides a marker from which to work-it is an artefact, but a useful one.

Because it is a scale with gradations, it moves away from perceptions of the problem as total and absolute, again creating the space for acknowledging difference. It provides a ready-made step by step approach to the solution, by identifying that the goal is 10, but accepting that it is possible to get there through smaller and more achievable interim goals. Asking people to provide a scaled number in relation to the problem, then exploring what the next highest number would look like, and how this might be achieved, either through their own actions and/or those of others, is more realistic and less daunting than going straight for the ideal state, which can appear so far distant that it is unattainable. When someone has clearly formed goals this is a useful tool for making a start. Where someone grades the problem at 0 or 10, it can be helpful to spread out the scale from 0–100. If 0 persists, then it may be useful to ask about the time when the problem was more than 0, as it is unlikely that anyone has always been in such complete difficulties. If 10 is selected, then the problem may well be solved and there is very little to be done, although it would still be an opportunity to explore how this has been achieved (Gosh, how did you do that?) so that the successful local skills and strategies can be used in future.

The motivation of the service user to enter into change is a key determinant of success in any intervention, as people may well be able to see a problem-free future, but because of their circumstances find it hard to begin to reach this state. Scaling questions can be used to ask people how motivated they are to engage with the process. For example, 'If 0 represents not being bothered to tackle the problem at all today, and 10 is absolutely committed to working' this can give some idea of where the person feels they are, and locating the feeling in the present allows for the possibility of change in the future. Again, using follow-up questions can promote motivation through; 'So you say you are at 2 today, what would you be doing differently if you were at 3 tomorrow?; When have you been at 3?; So you are not at 1, where has this motivation come from?', and thereby exploring what encourages motivation in order to *do more of it*. If people say that they are absolutely committed to working on the problem, 10 on the scale, then detailed questions can be asked about what it is that helps them be so strong in their motivation, amplifying and validating their reasons. A man who had been domestically violent said that he was *really committed to change and wanted to sort out his life*, placing himself at 10 on the scale. When asked where his enthusiasm came from, he was able to articulate that he wanted an end to his violence for the sake of his partner and children, as well as for his own peace of mind. A lack of motivation, or 0, can be clarified by asking what would be happening if they were at 1 on the scale, seeking clues to develop their motivation. A complete lack of identifiable motivation will indicate that someone is not *yet* prepared to change, and in some cases this may well lead to the imposition of controls, particularly where safety is an issue.

A further use of scales is in assessing confidence in the ability to work and to achieve the goals. The question: 'On a scale of 0–10, how confident are you today that you can reach your goals?' will indicate something about the person's motivation, and also provide opportunities to explore confidence-building. A self-assessment of 1 could lead to questions about exactly what would be happening if they were at 2; an assessment of 10 would warrant questions about where this confidence came from and how confident they are that they could maintain this. Confidence scaling is also helpful where there are others affected by the problem.

Practice Example 7.3

A man with learning disabilities who had been behaving badly at home was confident at 10 on the scale that he could change his behaviour and *get things sorted*. He was complimented for this, and asked how confident he thought his mother was that he could do this. He paused and then replied that he thought she would scale him at 3, so he was asked what he might be doing differently for her to scale him at 4. By asking follow-up questions he was able to develop more concrete actions to demonstrate his commitment to change to his mother such as talking nicely with her, keeping his appointments with his care worker and tidying his bedroom. When the mother was asked how confident she was about his ability to reach his goals she scaled him at 5 and was able to identify what he would be doing differently for her to scale him at 6, such as not putting himself at risk by staying out late at night, telling her where he was, not swearing every other word or not smashing the door in temper. From this, it was possible to develop ideas for tangible actions that would have meaning for all those affected by the problem, clarifying what expectations each person had to avoid confusion, especially where everyday communication had broken down.

Some SFBT practitioners have developed scale charts that are designed to assist people in thinking about exceptions to their problems and about their strengths. Milner and O'Byrne (2002b, pp. 179–186) provide examples of these based on the work of Kral (1989), Dolan (1998) and Lipchick (1988), and include their own lists that have been helpful in their practice. For example, they use the following scale chart with men who have behaved violently with women to allow them to reflect on their preferred way of being and what they may need to do to get there. The contents are based on discussions with women that Milner and O'Byrne know, but are not based on any large-scale survey or analysis; they are reasonable expectations of how someone should behave:

Scale for Getting and Keeping a Girlfriend (Milner and O'Byrne, 2002b, p. 184)

No.	Qualities women look for in men	Not at all	Just a little	Pretty much	Very much
1	Keep clean and smart				
2	Take her out (not necessarily expensive places – walks are fine)				
3	Holding hands				
4	Spoken TO and not AT				
5	Make her feel special (good manners, small gifts, cards)				
6	Cuddles (not necessarily leading to sex)				
7	Joint responsibility for contraception				
8	Make her laugh				
9	Show you are interested in her				
10	Not looking at other women when out				
11	Not expecting sex when you come home drunk				
12	Treat her as an equal				
13	Shared decision-making				
14	Give compliments				

15 (Add your own ideas)

16

17

The scale invites men to rate themselves in their interactions with women, encouraging them to think about what women want, rather than what they want or expect. It allows men to think about how they match up to women's expectations of their behaviour, as all the elements are actions rather than intrinsic qualities, and therefore open to change. If a man says that he keeps clean and smart *sometimes*, then this allows for follow-up questions about how he does this, when he does this, and how he can do *more of this* in the future. If he feels that he speaks *to* his girlfriend, but she feels that he speaks *at* her, then he can be asked to think about what he has to do differently for her to feel that he is speaking *to* her. The scale is wide-ranging and allows for at least some strengths to appear and it is unlikely that someone will rate themselves completely negatively. If they do, then this may indicate that they have a long journey ahead and that currently they may well be unsafe with their partner. Of course, if it is not possible to identify any of the elements then it raises questions about whether they have any meaningful relationship at all.

Scale charts do not provide a *scientifically* determined outcome that can be plotted into some algorithm and a score achieved. They provide useful material that can be developed through follow-up questions in order to assist people in identifying strengths and previous successes. 'When did you do that?; How did you do that?; If you were doing it a little, what would you be doing and how would you have got to the position that you were doing it?' and 'You do that really well, what does it tell you about yourself?' are all examples of follow-up questions that are positive and generate ideas for the future. Offering people the space to make their own contribution helps to indicate how hard they are prepared to work on the problem, what creative ideas they may have and also encourages ideas based on their particular and individual experience that will have specific meaning for them.

Sometimes, people find themselves in such dire straits that it is difficult for them to recognise or find exceptions to their presenting problems. Consider someone who has lost his partner and his children through separation, his job through redundancy and his house through repossession. It may be rather inappropriate to ask for exceptions to these events, as they are often beyond anyone's immediate control. This is also the case where people present with emotional distress following bereavement. In circumstances such as these, it is helpful to ask how people have coped with the loss in order to find those times when their local strategies have worked. 'How have you got by despite this dreadful situation?' acknowledges their feelings and presumes strengths in coping with adverse events. It allows for exploration of those skills people have in getting on with things at least some of the time, enabling discussion about how these can be used more often and effectively. Even though people may feel that the situation is as bad as it could get, it can be useful to ask what they have done to prevent it from being worse.

Exercise 7.2

- Make a list of the things that a professional people-worker does that tell you they are good at their job.
- Scale yourself about whether you do these things Not at all; Sometimes; Most of the Time or Always.
- Think about the things that you do Sometimes.
- When do you do these?
- What is happening when you are doing them?
- When was the last time you did them?
- How can you do more of them so that tomorrow you are doing them Most of the Time?

Chapter 8

Feedback and Subsequent Sessions: Evaluating Progress

Feedback

SFBT practice has recognised the importance of constructing helpful feedback for people at the end of sessions in order to build solutions. De Jong and Berg (2002, p. 128) identify three main aims of feedback:

- To assist in the development of clear goals
- To focus people on the exceptions that are related to the goals
- To encourage people to notice what they and others may be doing to make the exceptions happen

Taking a break from the session to think about what has happened and prepare for feedback is commonly used in SFBT. Some workers are able to go and discuss with colleagues, with the permission of the service user, to check out their understanding of what has emerged from the session, and to create clear messages. In some cases, the service user is invited to listen to this discussion between worker and colleagues in order to be as transparent as possible. The service user may find this strange as they are probably used to people making decisions about them, but as the discussion is simply about the content of the session and emerging solutions, there is no complex professional analysis imposed on this. The break gives space for both the worker and the service user to reflect on what has happened.

Milner and O'Byrne (2002b) have adapted Berg and Reuss's structure for feedback notes of the session in the following way:

- Problem description
- Exceptions and progress
- Thoughts on solutions
- Homework/tasks

This simple structure provides a comprehensive outline of the session that can be shared with the service user and can form the basis of case recording.

Tasks or homework are an often-used component of SFBT. Unlike many other theoretical approaches, the service user is the one who is the expert in their lives, and therefore change is not dependent on the relationship between the worker and service user nor is it limited to the session. Enabling people to find the skills and resources to pursue their own change in their own time is more empowering than assuming that the worker has to be there to lead, direct and control change.

Tasks can be suggested and negotiated and are focused on strengthening the exceptions to the problem. People can be invited to undertake concrete actions based on what has already worked, as *if it works, do more of it*. They can be asked to notice what is happening at those times when the problem is less of a problem, or when they are feeling more confident and capable, or when things are going well. Both these allow for reflection on difference away from the problem, encouraging an active role in this task for the service user. It can be helpful to ask service users to undertake pretend tasks. A boy who was not confident that he could change his problematic behaviour at home and that his mother would probably not recognise any efforts he made anyway was asked if he could pretend to be good on alternate days for a week, to see what reaction he got. Making this into a game actually reinforced his capacity to behave differently and to test out whether his mother would recognise the difference.

Further sessions: what is better?

Although SFBT accepts that interventions may only consist of one session, service users can, of course, return for further work. Solution-focused practice would encourage the use of the question 'What is better?' as this assumes competency and success, rather than questions such as 'How has it gone since we last met?' which invites stories of problems. The language used will lead on to various subjects, and SFBT wishes to go forward with problem-free talk, acknowledging that people have the capacity to effect change in their lives outside the therapeutic encounter with the worker. The purpose is to amplify exceptions and strengths. The majority will be able to see that some things have been better, although they may need encouragement to acknowledge this. Some will either say that things are the same or that they are worse. In these cases it is helpful to assist the person in detailing the time since the last session, asking them to think if there were certain times when things were better than others, for example if it was better in the morning or the afternoon; at school, work or at home; when they were in the house or out of it. Breaking down the time into components that can be compared opens opportunities to consider difference. If it was better when they were out walking, then this gives clues as to what might work in the future.

De Shazer (1994) outlines the purpose of subsequent sessions as being:

- Constructing the interval between sessions as including improvement
- Checking on whether what the client did in the meantime is seen as useful, inviting the client to see things as improved

- Helping the client to figure out what they have done that led to the change so that they can see what to do more of
- Deciding whether the improvements are good enough
- When no improvements can be found, working out how to do something different so as to avoid repeating what does not work

The Brief Family Center (Berg, 1994) has developed a handy acronym as a way of structuring these subsequent sessions; EARS. This stands for *E*liciting exceptions and strengths; *A*mplifying them; *R*einforcing them and *S*tarting again. The question 'What is better?' assists in the first. When exceptions are found then more detailed questions will be asked to amplify this, perhaps 'How did you do that?' As people often minimise their successes, this is a way of inviting people to say more about what they did well, which is an empowering way of validating them as the focus is on what they have done. Even small, overlooked successes can be important and they can teach us a lot about future strategies. Reinforcing is done through complimenting successes and strengths and enabling the person to see that they have the capacity to do more of this behaviour; that they can go some way to achieving their goals. Starting again may seem strange, but having identified some exceptions there is a strong likelihood that this may free someone up to further acknowledgement, so the question is 'What else is better?' This process can continue until multiple exceptions and strengths are identified that can be used to inform further actions.

Scaling progress and confidence

The scaling questions outlined in Chapter 7 can be useful in helping the person to think about their progress in achieving their goals. 'If 0 was the situation when you last came and 10 is having achieved your goals, where are you today?' This allows the person to share how they think they have progressed, and wherever they place themselves on the scale will allow for follow-up questions about what the next highest number will look like. This approach can be used to assess other people's perceptions as well, so if a man who has been violent scores himself at 5, his partner and children may rate him less than this. The discrepancy can be explored, and what he should be doing differently in order for others to rate him higher will be discussed.

Scales can be used to assess confidence, as people may be worried that they cannot sustain their progress given their previous circumstances and experiences. 'If 0 is not at all, and 10 is absolutely, how confident are you that you can maintain your progress and/or reach your goals?' Whatever people scale, further questions can be asked to clarify what they would be doing differently if they were at a higher score, and what gives them confidence. Both these questions elicit information about what works for them so that they can do more of it.

Relapses

As life is subject to change and rarely follows a straight and narrow path, service users may find that they have relapsed into the problem during the interval. This regression can be disheartening and feed into a sense of failure and hopelessness, both on their part and on that of the worker. However, within SFBT it is possible to use such setbacks constructively, based on the premise that by acknowledging a relapse it recognises that there are goals that have not yet been achieved; that a failure implicitly recognises that there is something which can be a success. Stories of failure require questions about the details of these events, particularly when lapses were not happening. If someone wishes to become drug-free, but admits that they have taken drugs in the interim, it is helpful to ask about the times that they have not been taking drugs; what was happening during this period when there were drug-free times. Rarely does someone present with completely ongoing problems, although it may feel that way. Asking on which days drugs were less of a problem than others provides material to think about how the person managed to avoid or reduce their use, so that they can find clues for doing more of this safer behaviour. Exceptions can be found that destabilise the totalising sense of failure, enabling people to recognise that they have a difficult problem, but that there is hope in combating this situation.

Endings

Solution-focused work ends when the goals have been reasonably achieved, or at least the path is clear enough to reach them confidently. Where there are concerns about safety and the impact of behaviour on others, then the perceptions of all parties should be gauged and people should be confident enough that the person has achieved the required change, linked to everyone's goals.

Exercise 8.1

- On a confidence scale of 0–10, where 0 is not at all and 10 is completely, how confident are you about using solution-focused approaches?
- If you were to rate yourself at the next highest number, what would you be doing differently?
- How would you have achieved this?
- What do you have to do to make this happen?
- What qualities do you have that will help to make this happen?

This section outlines some of the key points of anti-oppressive practice and then explores how solution-focused approaches can assist in achieving the aims of this way of working. Anti-oppressive practice encompasses a range of views and is subject to changes (Thompson, 2006), although some of the assumptions remain constant about the nature of social injustice and the moral imperative to act in ways that challenge discrimination and oppression. As many people who come to the attention of professionals and services will have experienced some form of structural disadvantage, it is important to recognise this and to reflect on how it may impact on their abilities to lead fulfilled lives, as well as accepting that we as workers are in positions of power and authority even though we may not wish to be seen as such.

Theoretical perspectives and practices play a part in questioning or accepting social injustice, with some theories having assumptions about the nature of people that reinforce socially influenced power relations. This section explores some of these complexities and outlines how solution-focused approaches can play a useful part in promoting empowerment at the point of contact between worker and service user, that is, at the inter-personal level.

Chapter 9
Anti-oppressive Practice Theory

The development of anti-oppressive and anti-discriminatory practice during the 1990s has been based on recognising the importance of structural disadvantage in the lives of people, rooted in a critical social scientific analysis (Mullaly, 1993). The differential impact of expectations of gender, class, race, age, sexuality and other ways of categorising people has had severe consequences for groups which have been marginalised within society, leading to the creation of *haves and have-nots*. Sexism, racism, ageism and similar factors permeate social, historical, cultural and professional understandings of the world, leading to practices that can be damaging, or at least neglectful, in realising that people's lives can be constrained by larger socio-economic forces. This critical approach was a reaction to the over-emphasis on the pyschologising of people in professional practice; practice that tended to locate the person as the problem without recognising their social, economic and political environment. For example, assessing someone as being *defensive* or *hostile* when they do not give answers to your questions may mask their negative experiences of previous professional power, or may be due to their perception of you as structurally advantaged by class, ethnicity or gender. We need to remember the nineteenth century US psychological diagnosis of *drapetomania*, which was proposed as the disorder that caused slaves to run away from their captivity. Rather than being an understandable reaction to oppression, running away was constructed as a mental aberration which could be cured. The social system of slavery was not criticised.

Dalrymple and Burke (1995), Thompson (2006) and Dominelli (2002) have been central writers in promoting the theorising and application of anti-oppressive and anti-discriminatory practice. Dominelli (2002, p. 6) provides a definition of anti-oppressive practice as:

> . . . practice which addresses social divisions and structural inequalities in the work that is done with 'clients' (users) or workers. Anti-oppressive practice aims to provide more appropriate and sensitive services by responding to people's needs regardless of their social status. Anti-oppressive practice embodies a person-centred philosophy, an egalitarian value system concerned with reducing the deleterious effects of structural inequalities upon people's lives; a methodology focusing on process and outcome; and a way of structuring social relationships between individuals that aims to empower service users by reducing the negative effects of hierarchy in their immediate interaction and the work they do.

Thus anti-oppressive practice is concerned with acknowledging the social origin of people's problems; the need to promote social change and the ways in which practice can be changed to take these into account.

The theory of anti-oppressive practice considers that the world is socially divided, with power being distributed unequally between these divisions. Burke and Harrison (2002, p. 229), say that: 'Social differences arise because of disparities of power between the dominant and dominated social groups. The major divisions are described in terms of race, gender, class, sexual preference, disability and age. Other differences, such as those of religion, region, mental health and single parenthood, exist and interact with the major divisions, making the understanding and experience of oppression a complex matter.' Thus in this concept there are key structural divides that lead to powerful and powerless peoples, for example white people have more power than black and men have more power than women, which allows the powerful group to oppress the less powerful. All these forms of oppression are destructive, leading to the abuse of the powerless, and those who are located at the powerless end of several spectrums are multiply disadvantaged.

When working with people we need to be aware of how these divisions may have or are affecting their lives, as their experience can severely limit their choices and opportunities. Indeed, people may well internalise some of the dominant images of themselves. For example, a disabled person may have absorbed the negative images of impairment to the point where they consider themselves to be of less value to society and their expectations of themselves may be constrained by this. The binary divisions also include worker-service user, nurse-patient or counsellor-client, where a professional role is viewed as being more powerful than the person receiving the service.

Anti-oppressive and anti-discriminatory practices have similarities, although there are debates about the different emphases within them. Both approaches recognise that we have to be vigilant that the ways in which we work do not compound problematic power relations in society and that we recognise the powerful position that workers inhabit. Indeed, workers need to be critical and reflective in their everyday practice to ensure that they do not abuse their position of structured power, as well as having a commitment to challenging inequalities. Burke and Harrison (2002, p. 230) say that this latter point is central because: 'Opportunities for change are created by the process of the challenge', although: 'Challenges are not always successful and are often painful for the person or group being challenged or challenging'. Challenging can often take a very direct form, confronting the use of oppressive language and concepts by workers, agencies and service users. Thompson (2006) states that practice is either supportive of inequality or questions it, using the political slogan, 'If you are not part of the solution, you must be part of the problem', to illustrate the imperative to work in ways that recognise the social and political context in which workers and service users find themselves.

A useful model in describing the multiple ways in which oppression operates is the *personal*, *cultural* and *social* (PCS) construct of Thompson (2006). This model proposes that the three domains each have sources of power that can be oppressive, and that these interact. The personal level focuses on the personal feelings, understandings and experiences of the service user and the relationship between them and the worker. Consideration needs to be given to the internalised oppressive attitudes of the person, which can include feelings of poor self-worth as in the example of the disabled person earlier, or it can be attitudes that are in themselves oppressive towards others, such as a domestically violent man who believes that women are inferior to him in status. The cultural level identifies the social norms that we are raised and operate in, exploring how they may support inequalities and provide the influences on the Personal. Broader structural contexts are also considered, for example the ways in which capitalism creates wealth and class divisions, how colonialism has determined racial hierarchies and how patriarchy has subordinated women to men.

Anti-oppressive practice theorists and practitioners are interested in how these different levels interact when considering the position of individuals. This leads to complexities, as multiple oppressions can make easy categorisation difficult. The experience of a black man will be different from that of a black woman; they both inhabit the category black, yet with different categories of gender. A white working class man may be structurally disadvantaged through economics, but experience this situation in different ways to a white working class woman. Indeed, it may be possible to *add up* oppressions that people are subject to in order to gain some sense of their lived experience.

Exercise 9.1

- Consider someone you have worked with.
- How many social binary divisions can you categorise them within?
- How have these categories affected their experience?
- How do you know this?
- How have you taken these categories into account in your work?

Chapter 10

Solution-focused Approaches and Anti-oppressive Practice

Healy (2005) identifies five key principles of anti-oppressive practice: A critical reflection of the self in practice; a critical assessment of service users' experiences of oppression; empowering service users; working in partnership and minimal intervention. This chapter maps how solution-focused approaches may assist in achieving these principles through practice examples.

Critical reflection of self in practice

In anti-oppressive practice it is important to reflect on who the worker is; what our values, attitudes and social structural attributes are that have combined to create the person we are today and how this may impact on our interactions with people. Awareness of membership of social divisions is seen as important, as these may have consequences that we are unaware of and may impact on how we are viewed by people. The limitations of membership of certain divisions are highlighted, for example the notion that we are unable to empathise with or understand the lived experience of people who may be subject to different social oppressions than we are. It can be very difficult for someone who is able-bodied to understand the situation of someone who is disabled or to truly enter into their lives to gain insight into their feelings, experiences and understanding of the world. Our category membership will influence the relationship with the service user (Burke and Harrison, 2002) and some of this will be based on assumptions about who we are, i.e. a professional, a man, white, through visibility by the service user, whereas we may make assumptions about who the person is through their obvious category as service user, disadvantaged, poor.

The focus on categories can lead to practices that are based on the idea that these categories are too distanced to be bridged, and that it may be helpful to provide a matching of a worker with a service user of similar social divisions. So a man may not be seen to be appropriate to work with a woman, or a white worker may not feel able to work effectively with a black service user. Conversely, it may be felt that it is effective to have a younger person working with teenagers, or someone may believe that they have a better understanding of disability because of their experience of caring for a disabled relative. All the above are based on notions that the categories are reasonably fixed and consistent, and that some oppressions can be used to give insight into others. It might be possible to reflect on your experience of racism as a black person to gain some understanding of how someone experiencing homophobia may feel. This creates some difficulties for those working with others, for example we often place people into obvious boxes of 'race', class and gender, but these boxes are not as rigid as they may appear. Obvious categories mask hidden ones, as sexuality, disability and religion may not be at first apparent. If someone is seen as a black woman, then practice may be based on this, despite her personal circumstances of also being disabled and lesbian. Matching, then, becomes a problematic exercise, as finding a worker for someone who has a whole range of equally important social division categories is going to be an almost impossible task.

Practice Example 10.1

At a conference organised at a university, a black, severely disabled woman was asked if she would like to select one of the group workshops that had been established. These were separate workshops for black people, disabled people, women, men and lesbian/gay people. She decided that as she was obviously black, disabled and a woman she would choose that day to join the lesbian/gay group, as this was the only category that other people would not automatically assume for her.

Privileging categories can also reduce individual people to a group identity, rather than recognising their personal and specific qualities and experiences (Fook, 2002). This is the case with workers, who may have a position of professional structural power as counsellors, youth workers, teachers, nurses, housing and social workers and so on, but this may be tempered in practice by service users who exercise power in other ways. There will be times when women readers have felt devalued by service users due to expectations of their gender, even though you may be a competent and powerful professional. The categories can tend to subsume differences within the social divisions, so the term black can be used to cover a whole range of non-white people who are incredibly diverse. This is not to presume that the category *white* is any more solid. In the UK today, for instance, this can include indigenous English, long-established Jewish, third generation Irish, first generation Polish and a host of other white peoples within this term.

It requires considerable skills to recognise and respond to these social divisions and their complexities, and rather than these skills being inherent in someone's experience or identity, they are skills that need to be learned if we are to work effectively with all the people we engage with. Solution-focused approaches treat categories with caution as being constructed in ways that can have a limited and situated benefit. For example, a child labelled with ADHD can receive substantial financial state disability benefits, and women's groups have played a strong part in raising problems about the oppressive behaviour of men and the way this is supported by social structures. The SFBT principles and practices outlined in previous chapters focus on the individual experiences of people, not ignoring the category they may inhabit, but seeking to enable the person to talk about their meaning of it and their personal ways of having successfully dealt with problems. SFBT does not make assumptions about people, apart from a relentless belief in the possibility of change, but will ask questions about their circumstances. Questions allow the worker to avoid making assumptions and judgements that are imposed- they provide the space for the person to tell you what it is like for them. Checking out that the questions asked are useful is perfectly acceptable, so 'Is what we are talking about OK, or should I be asking you something different?' helps to keep focused on the issues for the person.

Practice Example 10.2

Carl, a black teenager, was experiencing racist comments from other children at school. This was upsetting him and he had been verbally aggressive towards some children and teachers and was truanting from school. Action had been taken by the school which had punished the children involved in the taunting, but this had not diminished the problem. Carl rated his problem at about 6 out of 10 (0 being not a problem; 10 being the worst it can get). Carl was asked when the taunting was less of a problem, and was able to identify that there were times when he had ignored it and had also been supported by a group of friends who had been clear that they objected to the comments, when the problem had been about 4 out of 10. Carl was asked to describe in detail how he had managed to do this, and he outlined a process of stopping himself getting incandescently and uncontrollably angry, turning this into good anger after he had heard the positive remarks of his friends and felt better. He had then approached a teacher to tell them of the problem, and the teacher had immediately become angry themselves and confronted the taunting children, punishing them through detentions. Carl felt that he had lost control of this situation, as he had not wanted to escalate it to such an extent, which compounded his feelings of frustration and concern that the problem had only been superficially resolved for the benefit of the school anti-bullying policy.

Carl was complimented on his abilities and asked further questions about how he could use his skills of self-control and good anger to deal with the problem more effectively. He was able to recall times when he had not had a problem with the individuals who were taunting him and that it seemed to be only when they were in a group that the comments were made. Carl decided to avoid their group but thought he could probably talk individually with some of the children when the opportunity arose. He rated his chances of doing this successfully at 6 out of 10 (0 not at all; 10 completely successfully). When asked what he would be doing differently if he was able to rate it at 7, he was able to think about the way he would talk to them (respectfully but firmly) to improve his chances. As the children were

> Asian he thought that he could raise their experiences of racism to make them think about what they were saying to him. Carl was asked when the school had dealt with the problem more effectively, and he remembered when a similar problem had arisen and a particular teacher had listened to him and asked him what he wanted to happen. Carl felt that this gave him some say in the process and wanted this to happen in future. He did not feel able to discuss this with the school so it was agreed that the worker would do this with him.

SFBT encourages workers to hold back on judgements; to reflect on whether they have asked the service user enough questions to allow them to tell their story, rather than a story which has been interpreted through the values, experiences and professional knowledge of the worker. This helps to avoid making assumptions about people due to their group identity, and encourages reflexivity on the part of the worker. It is fine to ask 'Have I got this right, or am I completely wrong?' to ensure that the experience of the service user is acknowledged. Empathy is generated not by a non-professional shared group identity, but by ensuring that the person is heard and their unique qualities are recognised.

Of course, as in any therapy, there is the danger of becoming too focused on the individual and locating the problem as part of them. The previous example could have been extremely unhelpful if the problem behaviour was simply seen as located within Carl's responses. Seeking individual strategies to cope with intolerable situations is not the whole story; action needs to be taken on a broader level, which in this case included discussing his views with the school. A child, or indeed anyone, who is being bullied should not have to merely put up with this since solutions include structural as well as personal change, ensuring that the voice of the person is heard rather than assumed. Workers need to be vigilant against the individualisation of problems.

Critical assessment of service users' experiences of oppression

The PCS model of Thompson is useful in encouraging workers to consider the various structural factors that impinge on the lived experience of service users, including how these may shape and limit the choices and options available to people. Thinking about how the ways in which society is organised, which discourses are predominant and how these may work against people is an important aspect of understanding the situation many service users find themselves in. Such experiences can encourage people to view themselves as passive victims of circumstances, reduce their ability to take action and severely limit their life-choices. If a lone mother presents with depression and says that this is due to the appalling housing conditions she and her children have to live in, it would be pointless (and rather insulting) to explore with her the nature of her childhood attachments and how these have constructed her sense of self-worth. It is far better to recognise the injustice of such circumstances and to explore the ways in which the presenting problem can be tackled through engagement with housing services. A teenager who has been failed by the education system may have a restricted view of their own worth and have internalised some of the messages of *being thick*, possibly reinforced by unhelpful comments from teachers and parents. Problem schools are transformed into problem people, avoiding issues of under-resourced and inappropriate teaching demands.

In order to be effectively anti-oppressive, workers need to be aware of the potentially damaging effects of these experiences and be careful to avoid reinforcing these. The dominant discourses are often played out through language (Thompson, 2003), and the way people and problems are talked about can give subtle (and less so) messages about how the person is viewed. In contemporary society there is a general prohibition on specific, extremely offensive words that can be used, for example, about women, black people, lesbians and gay men in acknowledgement that such language reinforces negative images. Such words are of course to be avoided, but the language game is more complicated than these obvious targets. How we discuss a service user with other professionals can include normative and value judgements that may have the appearance of neutrality but actually reflect powerful positions that may be oppressive. Talking about black boys brought up by lone mothers as in need of *positive male role models* hides assumptions about cultural differences in child-rearing, ideas about gendered roles, the effect of poverty and racism on family structures and places the blame on the deficits of the family and black culture, rather than the social context. Stating that someone has not *come to terms with their disability* is also based on the premise that this is something that needs to be incorporated into a *true* identity for the person to recognise who they really are, rather than seeing disability as a complex interplay between bodily impairments and the social environment.

Language has also been critiqued by feminists as being man-made (Spender, 1985) and care needs to be taken in the forms of words used, which can be quite masculine when talking about *combating, beating, vanquishing* or other rather aggressive ways of describing dealing with problems. Use of language has informed some of the feminist criticisms of solution-focused therapy (Dermer *et al.*, 1998) and workers need to guard against linguistic structures that support a particular ideology. Accurately representing what people actually say is a way that workers can avoid imposing their own interpretations.

As SFBT is not interested in labels other than the meaning they hav and the exceptions to that label, it provides a way of avoiding the p tendencies of some models. Rather than seeking to confirm or theoretical hypothesis about who the person is, SFBT explores the l that people have of their experiences. This means asking questions do not already have an answer and waiting to hear what is said before formulating the next question, rather than having a pre-existing list to ask. Asking people 'Is the label an issue for you?' avoids making assumptions about the nature of generalised oppression. Milner and Myers (2007, p. 146) say that: 'Acknowledging an answer involves using service users' language, the actual words, and not translating them into 'practitioner' language'.

Practice Example 10.3

Jane was a lone mother who was struggling to look after her children due to a series of financial, health, housing and family crises. She described feeling crushed under the weight of her responsibilities, not having any time to herself and having to cope with a series of daily problems that included the increasingly out-of-control behaviour of her children and her feelings of being a bad mother. The solution-focused worker asked her to scale how good her life was at the minute, and she scored it 3 out of 10 (0 as the pits; 10 as the best ever). She was asked what made it 3 and not 2; what has enabled her to cope as well as she does with such a terrible situation. Jane was able to identify that she managed to feed the children, get them to school (most days) on time, keep them clean, not lose her temper with them all the time and she had a reasonable relationship with her social worker. She also shared her stress with a friend who she telephoned every day, managing to have a laugh about the Big Brother television show. The worker asked Jane how she managed to do all this given her situation, and Jane was able to give more clues about her skills at managing a routine, her financial management and cooking abilities, her cleverness at balancing the demands of different creditors, having a good moan to her friend about the social services and the times when she had kept her temper when faced with really bad behaviour by the children.

The worker then asked Jane that, given all the skills that she had described, how would she rate herself on a *good mother* scale of 0 (the worst ever) to 10 (the Virgin Mary)? Jane thought that she was actually about 5 on average, but there were times when she was 7 and others when she was 3. Jane was then asked what she was doing differently when she was at 7, and Jane said that she was more in control of her temper with the children, she was getting on better with the school, she was sitting down and sorting out bills, she was talking with her social worker less angrily and she used to have a night out with her friend once a week to blow off steam. Further detail was asked about how she did *controlling her temper*, how she *got on better with the school* and how she managed *to talk less angrily with her social worker*. These allowed Jane and the worker to think about how these strengths and exceptions could be reclaimed for future use.

The above example demonstrates how solution-focused work recognises and hears the subjective experience that Jane has of structural difficulties. By asking uestions about her specific situation, the worker was able to assist Jane in <ing through the complexities of her circumstances and in recognising that

there were some things that she could do and others that she needed professional support to address. To be *crushed* is a disabling situation to be in, one that reduces the opportunity to see strengths and exceptions, no matter how small. The above conversation generated a plan of action led by the service user. Clearly, she was at the sharp end of social expectations of women, of social policies that generate poverty and isolation, and professional agencies that do not always have the resources to eradicate problems. Jane would benefit from changes in policy that recognised the value of raising children and provided adequate financial means to do this, from questioning the assumed cultural role of women as providers, and from the deplorable state of much housing. However, Jane still has to deal with her everyday existence in the here and now, and waiting for structural change could take a long time. This is not to ignore the need for social action on a wider scale, and indeed there may be groups that it would be useful for Jane to join in order to challenge collectively some of these problems, but individuals require assistance in developing local strategies that will be helpful for them.

Empowering service users

The notion of empowerment is central to anti-oppressive theory and practice. Enabling service users to (re)gain greater control over their lives is a key element of this strategy, recognising that there are personal, cultural and social barriers to achieving this that need to be overcome. There are various ways in which this can be done. Dalrymple and Burke (1995) suggest that people should be encouraged to talk about their feelings of powerlessness, either with the worker and/or with other people who are experiencing similar difficulties. Mullaly (2002) outlines the need for people to become involved in *consciousness-raising* about the structural nature of their problems, which can help to reduce the personal feelings of inadequacy and blame, and lead to a recognition that they are not alone in their circumstances. Group work is seen as a powerful tool in this process, where sharing experiences can allow people to gain insight into the ways in which they are isolated, marginalised and oppressed, whilst providing the vehicle for collective action to challenge these problems.

Practice Example 10.4

Residents of a social housing estate created a group to campaign for improvements to their neglected environment. The group met with housing officials, local councillors, their Member of Parliament and the press to argue for better repairs, street cleaning and services for the inhabitants. The group was successful in gaining further resources and acted as a confidence-booster for members who had not felt able to take control of their situation previously. The group met at times suitable for the participation of as many people as possible and provided childcare to enable parents to attend.

The above example demonstrates the power of collective action in bringing about desired change, and will be a familiar (if idealised) story of empowerment. A solution-focused approach to such a group would concentrate on identifying strengths and capacities that may have been overlooked, rather than coming together to discuss defeats and examples of powerlessness. Mather *et al.* (2004) describe a solution-focused approach to group work with parents of children in care which illustrates this well.

The notion of consciousness-raising assumes that there is a political goal to achieve of personal change and it may take some time to question the often deeply held views of the person which are supported by social structures. There can be difficulties with this approach if the person does not accept the prescribed way forward, as this can lead to people being viewed as unwilling or unable to reach the desired state of consciousness, as having failed to see the *real* picture of their circumstances. Healy (2005, p. 190) warns that: 'The danger of consciousness-raising efforts is that those who do not conform to the truths presented by the anti-oppressive service provider may be dismissed as lacking critical consciousness or as conservative reactionaries'. This does not allow for a critical reflection on their practice and can over-simplify the complexities of power relations (Featherstone and Fawcett, 1994).

Practice Example 10.5

Sharon fled her home when her partner assaulted her after a drunken argument and she sought shelter in a women's refuge. She was invited to take part in group discussions about the nature of domestic violence, but found that she could not agree with some of the things that were said about men during these sessions, particularly about their propensity for aggression and control. Sharon's experiences with men had been complicated, with some individuals being kind and loving, whereas others had been violent, and some had been both. She felt increasingly isolated and that her views were being assessed as problematic, that she was not ready to change, and that she was in denial of the nature of the violence she had experienced. Increasingly unhappy, Sharon returned to her partner and the abuse continued sporadically for several years.

Anti-oppressive theory posits that service users are often restrained from empowerment through their lack of capacity and confidence, created by the disadvantages they have experienced. The need to recognise and develop strengths is a key element in empowerment that SFBT can assist with. Strengths perspectives have become increasingly popular within social care since the 1980s, having their roots in the work of Weick (e.g. Weick *et al.*, 1989) and Saleeby (1997) in the US. There has been criticism of an over-emphasis on problems which leads to accentuating the difficulties people face and does not provide for a good base on which to move forward positively. Solution-focused approaches can be located within a strengths perspective (Healy, 2005; McLeod, 2003).

Professional practice is increasingly regulated through government policy and the need to acknowledge strengths has emerged in the general and specific guidance issued for social work and social care interventions. Wheeler (2003), who has extensive experience of social care and has been instrumental in promoting SFBT in this context, identified that across a range of policy initiatives there has been an increase in commitment to partnership and in recognising the importance of the strengths people have, in order to produce the best outcomes for service users. The NHS and Community Care Act (DHSS, 1989a, para. 3.2.3) stated that 'assessments should focus positively on what people *can* and cannot do' (my emphasis). The Children Act 1989 (DHSS, 1989b) emphasised the need to listen to the wishes of children and families and this has been enhanced through subsequent research and guidance, for example with the *Framework for the Assessment of Children in Need and their Families* (DoH, 2000), culminating in the current *Common Assessment Framework for Children and Young People* (DfES, 2006). This explicitly states (para. 4.8) that the principles of the assessment should include:

- It is collaborative-you are working with the family to find solutions-they will often know better than you;
- You should consider the child's **strengths** [original emphasis] as well as needs and these should be recorded.

The guidance on the Single Assessment Process for Older People (DoH, 2002: Annex A, Page 2) suggests that one of the key attributes of any assessment is that it should be person-centred, and that specifically within this:

- The older person's views and wishes are central to the assessment process, and the assessment takes account of the **strengths** [my emphasis] the older person can bring to bear on their needs . . .

Within the range of services that social care workers operate it is clear that values of partnership, hearing the voice of service users, moving away from psychologising, considering the social context and recognising that in order to be empowered people need to be seen as more than just their problems, are being more explicitly articulated. SFBT can claim to be a way of implementing these policy imperatives through the focus on finding and developing strengths.

Weick *et al.* (1989, p. 354) consider this approach to be helpful for service users because:

> . . . a strengths perspective is a strategy for seeing; a way to learn to recognise and use what is already available to them. The professional person thus becomes a

translator who helps people see that they already possess much of what they need to proceed on their chosen path.

Thus an approach that searches for, and recognises, strengths is a useful tool for professionals, but one which requires thought in how it may be achieved. In many ways SFBT has provided a vehicle for achieving the aims of the strengths perspective, with a collection of principles and practice techniques that allow for the identification, validation, (re-)creation and application of those areas in people's lives that are working well. The SFBT emphasis on hearing the voice of the service user and ensuring that this is accurately represented, rather than mediated through professional language, is a way of avoiding marginalising people caught up in organisational structures, where it can be difficult to be heard in the forms, processes and multiple assessments that permeate social care practice.

Working in partnership

Partnership is a concept that is problematic within anti-oppressive practice, as the differential power distribution between worker, agency and service user is seen as enormously difficult to bridge. Thompson (2003) argues that the ways in which we communicate can assist in reducing this gulf, through being clear and open about why we are involved in people's lives, what we are doing, and how we are going to do it, including the authority we may have in our role. For example, most people-workers within statutory and voluntary organisations will have a child protection protocol which must be followed. It is important that service users are aware that confidentiality has limits and boundaries that will be acted upon should they be breached. Being clear about the restraints on your capacity to provide a service need to be acknowledged, as resources are often finite and your time will have limits.

SFBT is relatively straightforward to explain to people, unlike the complexities of other more structural and technological models of working. This aids partnership as it is empowering to know how workers are making sense of your situation, and is a way of sharing power; in this case the power of professional theoretical knowledge. Nothing is hidden from the service user in this process; meanings are not being inferred from what is being said, they are generated through the open process of talking. Written records of meetings are shared as there will be nothing in them that has not been already discussed. If the worker has reflections on the sessions then these will also be shared and checked for accuracy and usefulness. Recording is not a tool to take away and analyse privately, applying obscured theoretical perspectives; it is a description of what has happened, including agreed plans for the future, with ideas based on the exceptions, strengths and solutions within the discussion. The language used is the service user's and is respected.

Working in partnership is an aspiration for most people-workers, although it can be hard to imagine how this can work in cases where there is risk, danger and abuse. Turnell and Edwards (1999) developed an assessment framework based on solution-focused approaches for application in child protection, traditionally an area fraught with anxieties, problems and dangers. It is useful to consider how their *Signs of Safety* model works, as assessment is a key aspect of current professional practice and it demonstrates how solution-focused approaches can be applied in contexts where there are concerns about risks to vulnerable people.

Turnell and Edwards (1999, pp. 30–32) provide twelve key *practice principles* to develop this (the principles are original, the commentary has been modified).

Respect service recipients as people worth doing business with	Whatever the nature of the alleged concerns, the family need to be viewed as having the potential to change and to be partners in managing the problem. An attitude from the worker of hope and potential can affect the outcome.
Cooperate with the person, not the abuse	Working in partnership does not mean condoning the abuse. It is possible to listen to what people have to say and to assist them in developing change without minimising the abuse or colluding with them. Openness, honesty and treating people as individuals are key elements of this.
Recognise that cooperation is possible even where coercion is required	Workers have positions of responsibility for the safety of children and professional powers to enforce this. This does not mean that partnership is impossible, as coercion and cooperation can exist at the same time. Being open about your role and concerns is important.
Recognise that all families have safety	Abuse does not usually happen all of the time, and families will have strengths that can be used to build safety. Seeking these is useful.
Maintain a focus on safety	Increasing the safety of the child is the aim of the intervention. This needs to be central to all discussions and goals
Learn what the service recipient wants	Hearing what people want is important, and their goals can be used to develop safety, especially if they can be aligned with agency goals. If the service user is heard, then they are more likely to be motivated.

Always search for detail	Questions should be asked to elicit detail about the circumstances, as this allows for a richer understanding of the problems and the solutions.
Focus on creating small change	Ideal-state goals may not be easy or quick to achieve. Small steps and changes are important and need to be validated.
Don't confuse case details with judgements	Reserving judgement as long as possible is important, as this allows for further detail and information to emerge. Judgements are always tentative and contingent, and may be premature.
Offer choices	Imposing solutions may be required, but service users should be given as much choice as possible within this to develop their capacities.
Treat the interview as a forum for change	Assessment is not a static process of objective information-gathering. The contact with the family can in itself generate change and this needs to be recognised.
Treat the practice principles as aspirations, not assumptions	Working in this way is not always easy, and requires careful consideration and application. Child protection is fraught with uncertainty and it is not possible to get it right all of the time whatever the approach taken.

Turnell and Edwards provide a *map* to guide workers in applying the above principles in practice, what they call the six *practice elements* (p. 51).

Understand the position of each family member	The worker should seek to identify the values, beliefs and meanings that family members hold about their lives and the abuse, thus assisting the worker to maintain a focus on the uniqueness of the case and in developing local strategies that have more meaning for the family.
Find exceptions to the maltreatment	Searching for exceptions to the problem helps to create a sense of hope that the problem does not always exist; that the service user does have strengths that can be used to develop solutions, and that they can be empowered to do more of this in the future. Where

	there are no exceptions or they are not helpful, then direct coercion may have to be considered.
Discover family strengths and resources	Validate and highlight the strengths of the family that may have been overlooked or minimised. Child abuse is an emotionally fraught area that can freeze people into despair.
Focus on goals	Assisting the family to articulate concrete, meaningful goals that will improve the safety of the child and their lives generally is important. The goals of the agency also need to be well-formed and clear. Measurable timescales are useful, and the family's goals may be the most useful ones to work with, except where they contradict safety. A lack of goals is likely to indicate a lack of achievable safety.
Scale safety and progress	Identifying the safety and progress of the work throughout the intervention helps to assess change. This should include the perceptions of all individuals, including parents/carers, children and worker, which should be open and transparent.
Assess willingness, confidence and capacity	The family's willingness and ability to work towards solutions and safety should be determined before plans are implemented. A lack of willingness or ability would indicate concerns about future safety.

The above principles and practices provide an approach and structure that attempts to recognise the importance of trying to develop partnership in circumstances that are legally, morally and emotionally problematic, and where the safety of vulnerable people is at risk. The temptation to work in ways that are coercive in order to protect children is great, given the stakes involved. However, this approach provides constructive ways of recognising that families can develop solutions to problems through partnership and their local resources. It also provides a clearer view of the complexity of cases, including where the danger to children requires enforcement intervention. Even where children need to be removed from their parents, this process has the potential to at least be open, transparent and based on the specific details of that family, rather than an assessment that is imposed through checklists and pre-existing assumptions about the nature of families and individuals that abuse. It provides opportunities for empowerment within a potentially disempowering process.

Minimal intervention

Anti-oppressive practice recognises that any intervention in people's lives is fraught with inherent contradictions, with apparently benign intentions often masking social control functions. Anyone who works with people will have certain professional responsibilities that may lead to practice which may be helpful, but also controlling. An obvious example is that of child welfare, already discussed above. However, *all* interventions carry the possibility of oppression, either through agency requirements, personal values and skills, professional knowledge or lack of adequate resources. The notion that interventions should be as limited as possible underpins anti-oppressive practice, but of course this leaves open the question of what is the minimum *appropriate* intervention. In some cases, the use of authority can be helpful, such as when an older person is being financially abused by a relative, or when a man is being physically abused by his partner. Intervening with the authority to bring about change for the better can be positive, even though someone may feel that their choices are being limited. If minimum intervention is the desired state, then solution-focused approaches fit this principle as they are explicit in presuming brevity.

Minimum intervention is not the preserve of anti-oppressive theorists; it can just as well be harnessed to a right-wing agenda of the privacy of the family and reducing resources for people, or it can be seen as a helpful approach in preventing dependency, increasing independence and reducing reliance on external professional help. Long-term therapy is not always necessary (see Chapter 5), although some models of therapy presume that this is the case, which can lead to reliance on the therapeutic encounter as the source of change. SFBT assumes that intervention can be brief but also effective, enabling the person to generate their own plans, recognise their own strengths and see themselves as the expert in their own lives, thus placing them at the heart of the work and de-centring the role of the worker.

Part Four: Outcome Studies and Guide to Further Learning

One of the drivers in current professional practice is the need to demonstrate that interventions are effective, which is of course what any practitioner would want to aim for. As professionals we would aspire to working in ways that are helpful for people who are experiencing difficulties and adversity and we would also want to be sure that how we work has some support in research. Practice has to be justified to the service users, to ourselves, to our agency and increasingly to regulatory and external bodies, therefore this section will outline the emerging research evidence for the usefulness of SFBT in a range of situations and with people who present with a range of problems.

As this is an introductory book, there is a section on further reading and links that I consider to be helpful if you wish to pursue this topic. The suggested reading is a collection of clearly-written, accessible works that cover the range of theory and practice issues raised in the preceding chapters. Of course, the references provide more detailed and specific reading on the topics.

Chapter 11
Outcome Studies

Research into the effectiveness of practice is not without some conceptual difficulties and debates about the nature of evidence are currently rife. The Evidence-Based Practice (EBP) movement has promoted an agenda of rigorous application of natural scientific methodologies to understand the impact of interventions, claiming that this is the way to gain the truth of practice and to promote ways of working that meet the criteria for success (e.g. Munro, 1998). However, it has been argued that this approach, which is based on the modernist assumptions outlined in Part One of this book, cannot fully engage with the complexities of peoples' lives, as these tend to be rather messy (as any worker will attest to). Trying to bring rational scientific order to hugely complex situations inevitably leaves out some of the aspects that do not fit the model and there are problems with reducing people to components of their full existence, forcing them into research structures that produce a certain type of knowledge.

Taylor and White (2000) write about the need to introduce and value subjectivity in accounts of social care and health practice in order to have a clearer idea of what is happening, acknowledging that scientific methods can be useful in some circumstances but ensuring that a variety of approaches are used to assist in sense-making. Wampold (2001) rehearses the difficulties in applying natural scientific methodology to measuring the effectiveness of psychotherapy in general, raising questions about the ability of this method to be able to deal with the myriad of factors involved in interactions between the counsellor and those who are counselled. Theoretical models that claim to have *the* answer to problems, in both practice and research, should be treated with caution. As Parton (2000, p. 452) says: 'Uncertainty, confusion and doubt should form an essential part of any theoretical approaches which are serious about being used in practice'. This is not to say that nothing is helpful, but that we need to be critical of the way all knowledge is produced. The details of this debate are usefully and briefly outlined in Healy (2005) and leave us with questions about how we make sense of our interventions and recognising that there are several different ways of understanding *what works*, whilst remembering that claims about effectiveness are always partial, contingent and subject to change.

Whilst SFBT is a relatively new approach, there is, however, an emerging data base of studies that seem to indicate positive outcomes across various settings. MacDonald (www.psychsft.freeserve.co.uk) has created an on-line data base of evaluation studies for SFBT that is regularly updated and the European Brief

Therapy Association (EBTA) has a useful research section on its website at www.ebta.nu.

McKeel (2006) has produced an updated version of his chapter on research in Miller *et al.*'s *Handbook of Solution-Focused Brief Therapy* (1996). This usefully outlines the research background and specific studies relevant to SFBT. He begins with a caveat that many of the SFBT research studies are not located within the traditional rational-scientific approach of randomised control trials, comparison groups or experimental design; they tend to be more focused on the outcomes of the particular intervention in itself rather than compared with another approach. This creates some problems when there are demands for evidence based on such methods. Of course, the desire to apply natural scientific methods often neglects to acknowledge the limitations of these approaches, as science is privileged within our society. Nonetheless, there are studies that do have validity whilst having the humility to accept their limitations.

McKeel identifies a large and developing body of research that demonstrates the effectiveness of brief therapies, including work for people with severe and chronic problems. Comparative studies between longer-term and brief therapies have shown little or no difference in success rates (Koss and Shiang, 1994), although interestingly, most therapists tended to prefer intervention to be long-term, whereas service users start therapy with the expectation that it will be brief (Garfield, 1994). This probably reflects the preferred theoretical positions of the workers who conceptualise problems as being entrenched and therefore difficult to eradicate. Service users, on the other hand, seem to have more hope in changing their situation, something that is a useful resource in creating a problem-free future.

SFBT in different settings

Follow-up studies are useful in gaining some sense of how SFBT has impacted on the individual service users who have received the model. De Jong and Berg (1998) undertook a seven to nine month follow-up study of 141 clients at the Brief Family Therapy Centre who had received SFBT and found that 45 per cent had met their goal and 32 per cent had made some progress. Lee (1997) in a six month follow up found that 54.4 per cent had completely and 10.5 per cent partly met their goals. Macdonald identified 70 per cent success after one year (1994) and 64 per cent after three years (1997).

The range of problems that people present with has also been reflected in the effectiveness studies, with De Jong and Berg (2002) identifying that there had been a minimum 70 per cent success rate with depression, suicidal thoughts, sleep problems, eating disorders, parent-child conflict, marital and relationship problems, sexual problems, sexual abuse, family violence and self-esteem difficulties. This range of problems will be familiar to most workers. Parton and

O'Byrne (2000) were able to review the outcome literature at the time of publication and were impressed by the scope of the successes, which they were able to compare favourably with task-centred models. They chose task-centred work as it bears some superficial resemblance to SFBT and is a model that many workers say that they use.

In mental health contexts, Wheeler (1995) and Perkins (2006) found that it was effective with child mental health problems in a community setting while De Shazer and Isabaert (2003) reported that of 72 outpatients with alcohol problems treated with SFBT, 59 were either abstinent or controlled after four years. Eakes *et al.* (1997) found a marked improvement in the well-being of people with schizophrenia following SFBT compared to a control group of people who received traditional medical therapies. Interestingly, the SFBT group appeared to take more control over their illness than the comparison group, who relied more heavily on their pharmacological treatment and medical advice. If a definition of empowerment is being more in control of your life, then this demonstrated great potential for empowering service users in what has traditionally been seen as the domain of medicine.

Combating domestic violence is a key issue in contemporary professional practice and SFBT has a good and developing track record of responding positively to this, which counters some arguments that it may only be useful for somehow less serious problems. Milner and Jessop (2003) reported that 19 out of 20 completers of an SFBT programme for domestic violence had not re-offended after eighteen months and Lee *et al.* (1997) also found encouraging results in this area. Of particular interest is the low drop-out rate for this, whereas most programmes based on cognitive behavioural therapy (CBT) experience high rates of non-completion and base their successes on the smaller group which completes the programme. Tracking people who have had interventions is notoriously difficult, with people disappearing, moving on, dying or not engaging with the study, and most longitudinal studies of any intervention are beset by these limitations. Lee *et al.* (2003) managed to follow up 48 of the 90 people (male and female) referred to eight sessions of SFBT for domestic violence and found that after four years 17 per cent had re-offended, which is not high compared to studies of other interventions. Stith *et al.* (2004) found a very low recidivism rate after two years for those who had SFBT, compared with a control group where 50 per cent re-offended. Clearly, SFBT is not the panacea for all ills in the sense of a *miracle cure*, but it does seem to work for more people more of the time, even in cases of serious violence.

With children and young people, Newsome (2005) found an increase in social skills, classroom behaviour and completion of homework amongst pre-teenage children who had SFBT. The Junction, a Barnardo's Children's Service, is currently evaluating the effectiveness of SFBT with children and young people with sexually concerning or harmful behaviour, supported by the European Brief

Therapy Association. Provisional results are encouraging, with a low recidivism rate and good level of satisfaction with the service. Where professionals have incorporated SFBT into practice there have been positive results, with Sundmann (1997) finding that even where a limited use of the model was applied service users expressed more satisfaction with the service and were more engaged in developing joint solutions to problems. This was with a community-based social work team in an area of multiple and chronic deprivation with a wide range of socio-economic, physical and mental health, drug use, educational and emotional problems.

Gingerich and Eisengart (2000) reviewed the 15 controlled outcome studies of SFBT that had been undertaken at that time. They identified that five of the studies were very robust and showed positive outcomes. Four found that SFBT was better than no treatment or standard institutional responses to their problems, and one found SFBT to be comparable in success to a known intervention, that of Interpersonal Psychotherapy for Depression (IPT). The remaining ten studies were viewed as less robustly controlled but still indicated that SFBT was effective. At the time of the article, Gingerich and Eisengart were able to conclude that the studies they assessed provided support for the efficacy of SFBT, but did not permit a definitive conclusion. Macdonald (2006) summarised SFBT evaluation studies to 2006 and concluded that there had been five randomised control trials that demonstrated the effectiveness of SFBT, including three that showed success over other treatments. Eleven of the twelve comparison studies showed benefits of SFBT and one study was equivocal about the outcomes. The studies had included data on over 1500 people with a success rate of 60 per cent with an average of three to five sessions.

Research continues to emerge, but whether it will be able to meet the demands and expectations of positivist research methodology remains to be seen. There is some debate about the use of appropriate research methodologies for SFBT and the European Brief Therapy Association uses a protocol to assess whether a method is actually SFBT. In order to maintain treatment integrity (to ensure that the treatment is the same for everyone to enable meaningful comparison) they suggest the following elements must be present for it to qualify as SFBT:

- The first session must include the Miracle Question and a Progress Scale. These must be followed up by further questions and the client must be complimented at the end of the session.
- Subsequent sessions must begin with 'What is better?' and include a Progress Scale. These must be followed up by further questions and the client must be complimented at the end of the session.

In addition, further guidance is given about what sort of questions may be used in following up the initial questions. These elements constitute a pattern of activity that can be reasonably measured and demonstrate the aspiration of SFBT to be regarded as a mainstream therapeutic approach by engaging with dominant research paradigms.

How brief is brief therapy?

McKeel considers the evidence from research where the number of sessions has been recorded. Of 275 clients in the De Jong and Berg (1998) study each had an average of 2.9 sessions each. Macdonald (2005) followed up 118 clients in adult psychiatry (with an 80 per cent success rate) and found that the average for sessions was 4.03, with 25 per cent of the clients having had just one session. Shennan (2004) of the Brief Therapy Practice (www.brieftherapy.org.uk) identified an average of 2.7 sessions for families referred to a child and adolescent mental health service where there were significant self-reported improvements in a six to nine month follow-up. Across the range of studies it is clear that the number of sessions is remarkably low, particularly given the improvements and the range of problems covered. McKeel argues that there appears to be a correlation between the number of sessions and the success of treatment goals, with studies such as Macdonald (1994) showing that a good outcome had an average of 5.47 sessions, whereas service users who remained the same or became worse had received an average of 2.67 sessions. Of course, there are difficulties with creating an average from what could be a widely varying number of sessions, from a single one to whatever is required, and the lack of specificity about the *actual content* or *length* of the individual sessions, but the point remains that SFBT *can* be brief and still produce results.

Service user and worker satisfaction

Several studies show that service users find SFBT useful (Beyebach *et al.*, 1996; Metcalf *et al.*, 1996). They are able to specify the components of SFBT that are most appreciated, in particular the emphasis on finding their strengths and in listening to their stories. This is in many ways *doing respect*, although what service users like may not be confined just to SFBT but could be good values for any intervention. However, as what service users tell us they like about therapy in general reflect the central characteristics of SFBT, it is probable that this way of working has more chance of being of use than some other models. Research on the experience of SFBT with both men and women has shown little difference in outcomes. De Jong and Berg (1998) did a six month follow-up of 141 clients and found no significant gender differences in achieving goals.

Skidmore (1993), Sundmann (1997) and Bowles *et al.* (2001) evaluated the impact of SFBT on practitioners, who reported that the techniques were helpful and that they incorporated the principles into their practice. Myers *et al.* (2003)

illustrate this through conversations with practitioners who used solution-focused and narrative approaches in their work, reflecting on how these were helpful in constructing positive change and in generating a sense of hopefulness and enthusiasm in the worker.

Chapter 12
Guide to Further Learning

Useful websites

http://www.btne.org
The website for Brief Therapy North East.

http://www.brietherapy.org.uk
This is the useful site of the Brief Therapy Practice (BRIEF) in London.

http://btpress.co.uk
This is the publishing arm of BRIEF, providing lists of their own publications and other key SFBT and post-modern counselling texts.

http://www.focusonsolutions.co.uk

http://www.yorkshiresolutions.org.uk
The website of a group of SFBT practitioners who meet on a regular basis to discuss practice issues.

http://www.psychsft.freeserve.co.uk
This website has up-to-date information on research.

http://www.johnwheeler.co.uk
Wheeler has been influential in developing SFBT practice in social work in the North East.

http://www.ukasfp.co.uk
This is the United Kingdom Association for Solution Focused Practice (UKASFP).

http://www.solution-news.co.uk
The quarterly electronic newsletter of the UKASFP.

http://www.ebta.nu
The website of the European Brief Therapy Association. This organisation provides a forum for practitioners across Europe and beyond to share ideas, resources and research through an annual conference.

http://www.brief-therapy.org
Homepage of the Milwaukee Centre.

http://www.sikt.nu
Homepage of the SIKT solution-focused organisation in Sweden.

http://www.thesolutionsfocus.com
Homepage of Jackson and McKergow.

http://www.sfbta.org
North American organisation to promote and disseminate ideas about solution-focused work.

http://www.signsofsafety.net
Homepage of Turnell in Australia.

Key reading

Interviewing for Solutions, 2nd Edition (2002) by De Jong and Berg is a step-by-step approach to interviewing in a solution-focused way by two expert practitioners who have used their experiences to provide a comprehensive outline of the ways in which this method works. The book uses case examples to illustrate the key points of the process based on clients presenting with a wide range of problems.

Handbook of Solution-focused Therapy (2003) edited by O'Connell and Palmer, is a collection of contributions by authors working in a variety of different settings outlining how they have applied solution-focused practices. It is mainly located within UK organisations and is helpful to see how SFBT can be brought into a wide range of practice situations.

Guide to Possibility Land (1997) by O'Hanlon and Beadle gives good examples of how solution-focused practice can work in a straightforward and deceptively simple way.

The Solutions Focus: The SIMPLE Way to Positive Change (2002) by Jackson and McKergow is one of the most accessible introductory books to a solution-focused approach. It uses their particular emphasis within SFBT to take readers through the steps required to build solutions, with drawings and diagrams that not only inform but manage to amuse as well.

Solution-focused Therapy: Theory, Research and Practice (2007) by Macdonald, a psychiatrist, who has developed solution-focused approaches particularly for use within mental health services. He provides a comprehensive overview of the theory, with excellent examples of practice, and a significant evidence-base.

Social Constructionism, 2nd Edition (2003) by Burr is an excellent and accessible read about the development of social constructionist and post-modern ideas, with examples of how these can be applied to theorising practice.

Constructive Social Work (2000) by Parton and O'Byrne provides a clear and helpful outline of the theoretical influences on SFBT within this book, which synthesises solution-focused and narrative therapeutic approaches for social work practice. It makes the arguments about how social work needs to engage positively (constructively) with post-modern thinking to provide practices that are reflexive and responsive to individual need, whilst recognising the structural context in which service users find themselves. The use of language is well articulated in this.

Assessment in Social Work, 2nd Edition (2002) by Milner and O'Byrne includes a chapter on SFBT. The focus is on assessment and includes clear illustrations of how this stage may look using SFBT in a range of contexts. The chapters on other theoretical approaches allow the reader to consider the differences between various theory-informed practices, as well as providing some outcome studies for all the theories.

Brief Counselling: Narratives and Solutions (2002) by Milner and O'Byrne again looks at how solution-focused and narrative therapies can be combined in an effective way. The solution-focused element is clear and there are good discussions about the differences, similarities and utility of the methods.

Signs of Safety: A Solution and Safety Oriented Approach to Child Protection Casework (1999) by Turnell and Edwards describes the application of solution-focused principles and practices in an area fraught with concerns. They use the experience of introducing SFBT into an Australian child protection system and provide examples of how this approach can be effective and empowering where there is danger to children. Practitioners working in areas of public safety will gain valuable ideas for developing their practice.

Resolutions: Working with Denied Child Abuse (2006) by Turnell and Essex draws on the extensive experience of the authors in applying solution-focused principles and techniques to work with difficult cases where the situation is contested and complicated. Essex has been influential in developing such practice in the UK and has constructed creative and accessible exercises to aid working with children.

Working with Violence (2007) by Milner and Myers explores the range of practices involved in working with violence, including examples of how solution-focused approaches can be used effectively where danger and safety are key issues.

Anti-discriminatory Practice, 4th Edition (2006) by Thompson is the essential text for this approach, developing the ideas of previous editions in the light of contemporary debates about the nature of knowledge and emancipatory practice.

Endnote

Solution-focused approaches provide practices that can be helpful in a range of situations for people-working. The principles and assumptions therein promote an empowering philosophical basis that is translated into useful practices for assisting people to maximise their potential. Different elements of the approaches can be used wherever they may be appropriate; the approach does not have to be rigid, although this may be useful for some people (both workers and service users!). Grappling with the theoretical base can be a struggle, as it questions many of our cultural and professional ways of understanding the world, but it is possible to use the practices without an in-depth engagement with contemporary debates about the philosophy of knowledge, as the practices themselves are practical, accessible and reasonably straightforward.

I will leave you with some key questions for your further learning, based on the premise that *we are all in the gutter, but some of us are looking at the stars*:

Exercise 12.1

Imagine that in two years' time you have been awarded a special commendation from the service users you work with for being the best worker they have ever had:

- What do you think they would buy you to please you?
- What skills of yours do you think they would be celebrating?
- Which of those skills are pretty good at the moment?
- Which skills do you need to develop further in order to justify the award?
- When are you going to develop them?
- How are you going to develop them?
- What will the service users first notice is different about you when you begin to develop these skills?
- How will you know when you really deserve having the award presented to you?

References

Adams, R., Dominelli, L. and Payne, M. (2002) (eds) *Social Work: Themes, Issues and Critical Debates*, 2nd edn, Basingstoke: Palgrave/Open University Press.

Allgood, S.M., Parham, K.B., Salts, C.J. and Smith, T.A. (1995) 'The Association between Pre-treatment Change and Unplanned Termination in Family Therapy', *The American Journal of Family Therapy*, 23: 195–202.

Anderson, H. and Goolishan, H. (1992) 'The Client is Expert: A Not-Knowing Approach to Therapy', in McNamee and Gergen (1993).

Ansbacher, H.L. and Ansbacher, R.R. (eds) (1998) *Individual Psychology of Alfred Adler: A Systematic Presentation in Selections from his Writings*, New York: HarperCollins.

Bateson, G. (1972) (ed.) *Steps to an Ecology of Mind: Collected Essays in Anthropology, Psychiatry, Evolution and Epistemology*, New York: Ballantine.

Bauman, Z. (1993) *Postmodern Ethics*, Cambridge: Polity Press.

Beckett, C. (2006) *Essential Theory for Social Work Practice*, London: Sage.

Berg, I.K. (1994) *Family Based Services: A Solution-Focused Approach*, New York; W.W. Norton.

Berg, I.K. and Miller, S.D. (1992) *Working with the Problem Drinker: A Solution-Focused Approach*, New York: W.W. Norton.

Berg, I.K. and Reuss, N.H. (1998) *Solutions, Step by Step. A Substance Abuse Treatment Manual*, New York: W.W. Norton.

Berger, P. and Luckman, T. (1967) *The Social Construction of Reality: A Treatise in the Sociology of Knowledge*, New York: Doubleday.

Bergin, A.E. and Garfield, S.L. (2003) (eds) *Handbook of Psychotherapy and Behaviour Change: An Emperical Analysis*, 4th edn, New York: Wiley.

Besley, A.C. (2002) 'Foucault and the Turn to Narrative Therapy', *British Journal of Guidance and Counselling*, 30 (2) 125–43.

Beyebach, M., Morejon, A.R., Palenzuela, D.L. and Rodriguez-Aries, J.L. (1996) 'Research on the Process of Solution-Focused Therapy', in Miller, Hubble and Duncan (1996).

Biestek, F.P. (1957) *The Casework Relationship*, Chicago: Loyola University Press.

Bowlby, J. (1951) *Child Care and the Growth of Love*, Geneva: World Health Organisation.

Bowlby, J. (1988) *A Secure Base: Clinical Applications of Attachment Theory*, London: Routledge.

Bowles, N., Mackintosh, C. and Torn, A. (2001) 'Nurses' Communication Skills: An Evaluation of the Impact of Solution Focused Communication Training', *Journal of Advanced Nursing*, 36: 347–54.

Burke, B. and Harrison, P. (2002) *Anti-oppressive Practice*, in Adams, Dominelli and Payne (2002).

Burr, V. (2003) *Social Constructionism*, London: Routledge.

Butt, T. (2004) *Understanding People*, Basingstoke: Palgrave.

Capaccione, L. (1979) *The Creative Journal: The Art of Finding Yourself*, Athens, OH: Ohio University/Swallow Press.

Cox, L. and Campbell, A. (2003) 'Let's Live, and See: Interview with Moshe Talmon', *Australian and New Zealand Journal of Family Therapy*, 24 (1) 38–40.

Dalrymple, J. and Burke, B. (1995) *Anti-Oppressive Practice: Social Care and the Law*, Buckingham: Open University Press.

De Jong, P. and Berg, I.K. (2002) *Interviewing for Solutions*, 2nd edn, Brookes/Cole: Pacific Heights, CA.

Dermer, S.B., Hemesath, C.W. and Russell, C.S. (1998) 'A Feminist Critique of Solution-focused Therapy, *American Journal of Family Therapy*, 26: 239–250.

Derrida, J. (1982) *Margins of Philosophy* (Translation and Annotation by Alan Bass). Chicago: University of Chicago Press.

De Shazer, S. (1982) *Patterns of Brief Family Therapy*, New York: Guilford.

De Shazer, S. (1984) 'The Death of Resistance', *Family Process*, 23: 11–21.

De Shazer, S. (1985) *Keys to Solutions in Brief Therapy*, New York and London: W.W. Norton.

De Shazer, S. (1988) *Clues: Investigating Solutions in Brief Therapy*, New York and London: W.W. Norton.

De Shazer, S. (1991) *Putting Difference to Work*, New York and London: W.W. Norton.

De Shazer, S. (1993) 'Vive la Difference', in Gilligan, S. and Price, R. (eds) *Therapeutic Conversations*.

De Shazer, S. (1994) *Words Were Originally Magic*, New York and London: W.W. Norton.

De Shazer, S., Berg, I.K., Lipchik, E., Nunnaly, E., Molnar, A., Gingerich, W. and Weiner-Davies, M. (1986) 'Brief Therapy: Focused Solution Development', *Family Process*, 25: 207–21.

De Shazer, S. and Isebaert, L. (2003) 'The Bruges Model: A Solution-focused Approach to Problem Drinking', *Journal of Family Psychotherapy*, 14: 43–52.

DfES (2006) *The Common Assessment Framework for Children and Young People: Practitioners' Guide*. London: HMSO.

DHSS (1989a) *Caring for People: Community Care in the Next Decade and Beyond*, London: HMSO.

DHSS (1989b) *The Children Act*. London: HMSO.

DoH (2002) *The Single Assessment Process: Guidance for Local Implementation: Annexes to Guidance*. London: HMSO.

Dolan, Y. (1991) *Resolving Child Abuse: Solution-Focused Therapy and Ericksonian Hypnotherapy for Adult Survivors*, New York: W.W. Norton.

Dolan, Y. (1998) *One Small Step: Moving Beyond Trauma to a Life of Joy*, Watsonville, CA: Papier-Mache Press.

Dominelli, L. (2002) *Anti-oppressive Social Work: Theory and Practice*, Basingstoke: Open University Press.

Durrant, M. (1993) *Residential Treatment: A Cooperative Competency Approach to Therapy and Programme Design*, New York: W.W. Norton.

Eakes, G., Walsh, S., Markowski, M., Cain, H. and Swanson, M. (1997) 'Family-centred Brief Solution-focused Therapy with Chronic Schizophrenia: A Pilot Study', *Journal of Family Therapy*, 19: 145–58.

Egan, G. (1998) *The Skilled Helper*, Monterey, CA: Brooks/Cole.

Erickson, M.H. and Rossi, E. (1980) *Innovative Hypnotherapy: Collected Papers of Milton Erickson on Hypnosis*, New York: Irvington.

Erikson, E.H. (1948) *Children and Society*, Harmondsworth: Penguin.

Featherstone, B. and Fawcett, B. (1994) 'Feminism and Child Abuse: Opening up some Possibilities?' *Critical Social Policy*, 14 (3) 61–80.

Fook, J. (2002) *Social Work: Critical Theory and Practice*, London: Sage.

Foucault, M. (1988) *Politics, Philosophy, Culture: Interview and other Writings 1977–1984*, New York: Routledge.

Freud, S. (1952) *Collected Papers, 1917*, (Translated by J. Riviere Vol. 1V), London: Hogarth Press.

Furman, B. and Ahola, T. (1992) *Solution Talk: Hosting Therapeutic Conversations*, New York and London: W.W. Norton.

Garfield, S.L. (1994) 'Research on Client Variables in Psychotherapy', in Bergin and Garfield (2003).

George, E., Iveson, C. and Ratner, H. (2000) *Solution Focused Brief Therapy Course Notes*, London: Brief Therapy Practice.

Gergen, K.J. (1985) 'The Social Constructionist Movement in Modern Psychology', *American Psychologist*, 40: 266–75.

Gilligan, S.G. and Price, R. (1993) (eds) *Therapeutic Conversations*, New York: W.W. Norton.

Gingerich, W.J. and Eisengart, S. (2000) 'Solution-Focused Brief Therapy: A Review of the Outcome Research', *Family Process*, 39 (4) 477–98.

Greene, G.J. and Kondrat, D.C. (2006) 'A Solution-focused Approach to Case Management and Recovery with Consumers who have a Severe Mental Disability', *Families in Society: The Journal of Contemporary Human Services*, 87 (3) 339–51.

Haley, J. (1967) (ed.) *Advanced Techniques of Hypnosis and Therapy: Selected Papers of Milton Erickson M. D.*, New York: Grune and Stratton.

Hawkes, D. (2003) 'A Solution Focused Approach to "Psychosis"', in O'Connell and Palmer, (2003).

Healey, K. (2005) *Social Work Theories in Context: Creating Frameworks for Practice*, Basingstoke: Palgrave.

Hubble, M.L., Duncan, B.L. and Miller, S.D. (1999) *The Heart and Soul of Change: What Works in Therapy*, Washington DC: American Psychological Association.

Jackson, P.Z. and McKergow, M. (2002) *The Solutions Focus: The Simple Way to Positive Change*. London: Nicolas Brearley Publishing.

Jacob, E. (2001) *Solution Focused Recovery from Eating Distress*, London: B.T. Press.

Johnson, L.N., Nelson, T.S. and Allgood, S.M. (1998) 'Noticing Pre-treatment Change and Therapeutic Outcome: An Initial Study', *The American Journal of Family Therapy*, 26: 159–68.

Jordan, K. (2001) 'Briefer than Brief Therapy: A Response to Today's Managed Care Demands Combining Programmed Distance Writing Assignments with Brief Therapy', *Journal of Systemic Therapies*, 20 (4): 67–80.

Korman, H. (2004) *The Common Project*, http/:www.sikt.nu/ArticL_and_book/Creating%20a%20common%20project.pdf

Koss, M.P. and Shiang, J. (1994) 'Research on Brief Psychotherapy', in Bergin and Garfield (2003).

Kral, R. (1989) *Strategies that Work: Techniques for Solutions in the Schools*, Milwaukee, WI: Brief Family Therapy Centre.

Kutash, I.L. and Wolf, A. (1986) (eds) *Psychotherapist's Casebook: Theory and Techniques in the Practice of Modern Therapies*, San Francisco: Jossey-Bass.

Lambert, M.J. and Bergin, A.E. (1994) 'The Effectiveness of Psychotherapy', in Bergin and Garfield (2003).

Lee, M-Y. (1997) 'The Study of Solution Focused Brief Family Therapy: Outcomes and Issues', *American Journal of Family Therapy*, 25 (1) 3–17.

Lee, M-Y., Greene, G.J., Uken, A., Sebold, J. and Rheinshold, J. (1997) 'Solution-focused Brief Group Treatment: A Viable Modality for Domestic Violence Offenders?' *Journal of Collaborative Therapies*, 4: 10–17.

Lee, M-Y., Sebold, J. and Uken, A. (2003) *Solution Focused Treatment of Domestic Violence Offenders*. New York: Oxford University Press.

Lethem, J. (2002) 'Brief Solution Focused Therapy', *Child and Adolescent Mental Health*, 7 (4) 189–92

Lipchik, E. (1994) 'The Rush to be Brief', *Networker*, March/April: 35–9.

Lipchik, E. (1988) 'Purposeful Sequences for Beginning the Solution-Focused Interview', in Lipchik (ed.) *Interviewing*. Rockville, MD: Aspen.

Lipchick, E. (1988) (ed.) *Interviewing*, Rockville, MD: Aspen.

Macdonald, A.J. (1994) 'Brief Therapy in Adult Psychiatry', *Journal of Family Therapy*, 16: 415–26.

Macdonald, A.J. (1997) 'Brief Therapy in Adult Psychiatry: Further Outcomes', *Journal of Family Therapy*, 19: 213–22.

Macdonald, A.J. (2005) 'Brief Therapy in Adult Psychiatry: Results from 15 Years of Practice, *Journal of Family Therapy*, 27: 65–75.

Macdonald, A. (2007) *Solution-Focused Therapy: Theory, Research and Practice*, London: Sage.

Maller, L., Barber, L. and the Parents of the Connecting Parenting Play Group (2004) 'Climbing the Mountain', *International Journal of Narrative Therapy and Community Work*, 4: 13–22.

McAllister, M. and Moyle, W. (2006) 'Applying the Principles and Techniques of Solution-focused Therapy to Career Counselling', *Counselling Psychology Quarterly*, 19 (2) 189–203.

McKeel, J. (2006) *A Selected Review of Research of Solution Focused Brief Therapy*. www.psychsft.freeserve.co.uk/mckeel.htm.

McLeod, J. (2003) *An Introduction to Counselling*, 3rd edn, Maidenhead: Open University Press.

McMahon, M.O. (1996) *The General Method of Social Work Practice: A Problem-solving Approach*, 3rd edn, Boston: Allyn and Bacon.

McNamee, S. and Gergen, K.J. (1993) (eds) *Therapy as Social Construction*, Newbury Park, CA: Sage.

Metcalf, L., Thomas, F.N., Miller, S.D. and Hubble, M.A. (1996) 'What Works in Solution-Focused Brief Therapy', in Miller, Hubble and Duncan (1996).

Miller, G. (1997) *Becoming Miracle Workers: Language and Meaning in Brief Therapy*, New York: Aldine De Gruyter.

Miller, G. and De Shazer, S. (2000) 'Emotions in Solution Focused Therapy: A Re-examination', *Family Process*, 39: 5–23.

Miller, S.D. and Berg, I.K. (1995) *The Miracle Method*, New York: W.W. Norton.

Miller, S.D., Hubble, M.A. and Duncan, B.L. (eds) (1996) *Handbook of Solution-Focused Brief Therapy*, San Francisco: Jossey-Bass.

Milner, J. (2001) *Women and Social Work: Narrative Approaches*, Basingstoke: Palgrave.

Milner, J. and Jessop, D. (2003) 'Domestic Violence: Narratives and Solutions', *Probation Journal*, 50: 127–141.

Milner, J. and Myers, S. (2007) *Working with Violence*, Basingstoke: Palgrave.

Milner, J. and O'Byrne, P. (2002a) *Assessment in Social Work*, 2nd edn, Basingstoke: Palgrave.

Milner, J. and O'Byrne, P. (2002b) *Brief Counselling: Narratives and Solutions*, Basingstoke: Palgrave.

Milner, J. and O'Byrne, P. (2004) *Assessment in Counselling: Theory, Process and Decision-Making*, Basingstoke: Palgrave.

Mullaly, R. (1993) *Structural Social Work: Ideology, Theory and Practice*, Toronto: McCleland and Stewart.

Mullaly, B. (2002) *Challenging Oppression: A Critical Social Work Approach*, Ontario: Oxford University Press.

Munro, E. (1998) *Understanding Social Work: An Empirical Approach*, London: Athlone Press.

Myers, S., McLaughlin, M. and Warwick, K. (2003) 'The Day the Touching Monster Came: Narrative and Solution Focused Approaches to Working with Children with Sexually Inappropriate Behaviour', *Journal of Educational Psychology*, 20: 76–89.

Newsome, W.S. (2005) 'The Impact of Solution Focused Brief Therapy with At-Risk Junior High School Students', *Children and Schools*, 87: 83–91.

Nylund, D. and Corsiglia, V. (1994) 'Becoming Solution Focused in Brief Therapy: Remembering Something Important we already Knew', *Journal of Systemic Therapies*, 13 (1) 5–12.

O'Connell, B. (1998) *Solution Focused Therapy*, London: Sage.

O'Connell, B. (2001) *Solution-focused Stress Counselling*, London: Continuum.

O'Connell, B. (2003) 'Introduction to the Solution Focused Approach', in O'Connell and Palmer (2003).

O'Connell, B. and Palmer, S. (2003) (eds) *Handbook of Solution-focused Therapy (Brief Therapies)*, London: Sage Publications.

O'Hanlon, B. (1993) 'Possibility Therapy', in Gilligan and Price (1993).

O'Hanlon, B. (1995) *Breaking the Bad Trance*. London Conference entitled ''Breaking the Bad Trance'.

O'Hanlon, B. and Beadle, S. (1997) *Guide to Possibility Land: Fifty-One Methods for Doing Brief, Respectful Therapy*. New York: W.W. Norton.

O'Hanlon, W.H. and Weiner-Davies, M. (1988) *In Search of Solutions: A New Direction in Psychotherapy*. New York: W.W. Norton.

Parton, N. (2000) 'Some Thoughts on the Relationship between Theory and Practice in and for Social Work', *British Journal of Social Work*, 30: 449–63.

Parton, N. and O'Byrne, P. (2000) *Constructive Social Work: Towards a New Practice*, Basingstoke: Macmillan.

Payne, M. (2006) *Narrative Therapy; An Introduction for Counsellors*, 2nd edn, London: Sage.

Perkins, R. (2006) 'The Effectiveness of One Session of Therapy using a Single-Session Therapy Approach for Children and Adolescents with Mental Health Problems', *Psychology and Psychotherapy: Theory, Research and Practice*, 79 (2) 215–27.

Peters, M.A. (1999) '(Posts-) Modernism and Structuralism: Affinities and Theoretical Innovations'. *Sociological Research Online*, 3 (September), www.socresonline.org.uk/4/3/peters.html.

Potter, J. and Wetherell, M. (1987) *Discourse and Social Psychology; Beyond Attitudes and Behaviour*, London: Sage.

Rogers, C.R. (1957) 'The Necessary and Sufficient Conditions for Therapeutic Personality Change', *Journal of Counselling Psychology*, 21: 95–103.

Rogers, C.R. (1986) 'Client-Centered Therapy', in Kutash and Wolf (1986).

Rorty, R. (ed.) (1967) *The Linguistic Turn: Recent Essays in Philosophical Method*, Chicago: University of Chicago Press.

Rorty, R. (1979) *Philosophy and the Mirror of Nature*, Princeton: Princeton University Press.

Rosenau, P.M. (1992) *Post-Modernism and the Social Sciences: Insights, Inroads and Intrusions*. Princeton, NJ: Princeton University Press.

Saleeby, D. (1997) (ed.) *The Strengths Perspective in Social Work Practice*, 2nd edn, New York: Longman.

Sharry, J., Madden, B. and Darmody, M. (2003) *Becoming a Solution Detective*, Binghampton, NY: Haworth Press.

Sheldon, B. (1995) *Cognitive Behavioural Therapy: Research, Practice and Philosophy*, London and New York: Routledge.

Shennan, G. and Hacket, P. (2004) *Doing Solution Focused Work with Families*. Workshop at the European Brief Therapy Conference, Amsterdam, September 2004.

Sinclair, R., Garrett, L. and Berridge, D. (1995) *Social Work Assessment with Adolescents*, London: NCB.

Skidmore, J.E. (1993) *A Follow-up of Therapists Trained in the Use of the Solution-Focused Brief Therapy Model*, Doctoral Dissertation: University of South Dakota.

Smart, B. (1999) *Facing Modernity: Ambivalence, Reflexivity and Morality*, London: Sage.

Spender, D. (1985) *Man Made Language*, 2nd edn, London: Routledge.

Stith, S.M., Rosen, K.H., McCollum, E.E. and Thomsen, C.J. (2004) 'Treating Intimate Partner Violence with Intact Couple Relationships: Outcomes of Multi-couple versus Individual Couple Therapy', *Journal of Marital and Family Therapy*, 30: 305–18.

Sundmann, P. (1997) 'Solution Focused Ideas in Social Work', *Journal of Family Therapy*, 19: 159–72.

Taylor, C. and White, S. (2000) *Practising Reflexivity in Health and Welfare: Making Knowledge*, Buckingham: Open University Press.

Thompson, N. (2003) *Language and Communication*, Basingstoke: Palgrave.

Thompson, N. (2006) *Anti-Discriminatory Practice*, 4th edn, Basingstoke: Palgrave.

Turnell, A. and Lipchick, E. (1999) 'The Role of Empathy in Brief Therapy: The Overlooked but Vital Context', *Australia and New Zealand Journal of Family Therapy*, 20 (4) 177–182.

Turnell, A. and Edwards, S. (1999) *Signs of Safety: A Solution and Safety Oriented Approach to Child Protection Casework*. New York: W.W. Norton.

Turnell, A. and Essex, S. (2006) *Resolutions: Working with 'Denied' Child Abuse*. Buckingham: Open University Press.

Vinnicombe, G. (2004) *Greg's SFBT Handout*. www.yorkshiresolutions.org.uk/download/04-08GregSevenPages.doc (Accessed 04.01.06).

Wampold, B.E. (2001) *The Great Psychotherapy Debate: Models, Methods and Findings*. Mahwah, NJ: Lawrence Erlbaum.

Warner, R.E. (1994) 'Counsellor Bias against Shorter Term Counselling? A Comparison of Counsellor and Client Satisfaction in a Canadian Setting', *International Journal for the Advancement of Counselling*, 18: 153–62.

Warner, S. (2001) 'Disrupting Identity through Visible Therapy: A Feminist Post-structuralist Approach to Working with Women who have Experienced Child Sexual Abuse', *Feminist Review*, 68: 115–39.

Weakland, J.H. and Jordan, L. (1992) 'Working Briefly with Reluctant Clients: Child Protective Services as an Example'. *Journal of Family Therapy*, 14: 231–54.

Weick, A., Rapp, C., Sullivan, P. and Kisthardt, W. (1989) 'A Strengths Perspective for Social Work Practice', *Social Work*, July: 350–54.

Wheeler, J. (1995) 'Believing in Miracles: The Implications and Possibilities of Using Solution-Focused Therapy in a Child Mental Health Setting', *ACPC Reviews and Newsletter*, 17: 255–61.

Wheeler, J. (2003) 'Solution-focused Practice in Social Work', in O'Connell, B. and Palmer, S. (2003).

White, M. and Epston, D. (1990) *Narrative Means to Therapeutic Ends*. New York and London: W.W. Norton.

Wittgenstein, L. (1963) *Philosophical Investigations*, Oxford: Blackwell.

Index

 Theory into Practice

Other books in this series include:

Religion and Spirituality
By Bernard Moss

978-1-903855-57-7   2005

Values
By Bernard Moss

978-1-903855-89-8   2007

Power and Empowerment
By Neil Thompson

978-1-903855-99-7   2007

Age Discrimination
By Sue Thompson

978-1-903855-59-1   2005

Community Care
By Neil Thompson and Sue Thompson

978-1-903855-58-4   2005

Safeguarding Adults
By Jackie Martin

978-1-905541-98-0   2007

Full details can be found at www.russellhouse.co.uk and we are always pleased to send out information to you by post.
Our contact details are at the front of this book.